WILLIAMS-SONOMA

SOUP & STEW

RECIPES
DIANE ROSSEN WORTHINGTON

GENERAL EDITOR
CHUCK WILLIAMS

PHOTOGRAPHS
MAREN CARUSO

SIMON & SCHUSTER • SOURCE

NEW YORK • LONDON • TORONTO • SYDNEY • SINGAPORE

CONTENTS

THE CLASSICS

SIMPLE SOUPS

FIRST-COURSE SOUPS

MAIN-COURSE SOUPS

HEARTY STEWS

BRAISES

INTRODUCTION

Simmering a melange of ingredients in the soup pot is an ancient approach to cooking, and always results in a delicious melding of flavors. Each country's cuisine has its own treasured national specialties, from Russian borscht to traditional French white bean and sausage stew to Chinese wonton soup. Versatile and satisfying, soups and stews are perfect for many occasions. A simple cream of tomato soup provides a wonderfully easy weeknight dinner, while a hearty main-course stew or chowder is guaranteed to please a hungry crowd.

The best soups and stews from around the world are shared in the pages of this book. A bonus chapter of savory braises takes stews to the next level by simmering larger pieces of poultry or meat for an incomparably savory result. Some dishes are quick and easy while others take time to slowly develop flavor. At the end of the book, a section on basic techniques provides what you need to know. Once you have tried some of the superb recipes in this volume, I am sure that they will quickly become favorites in your home.

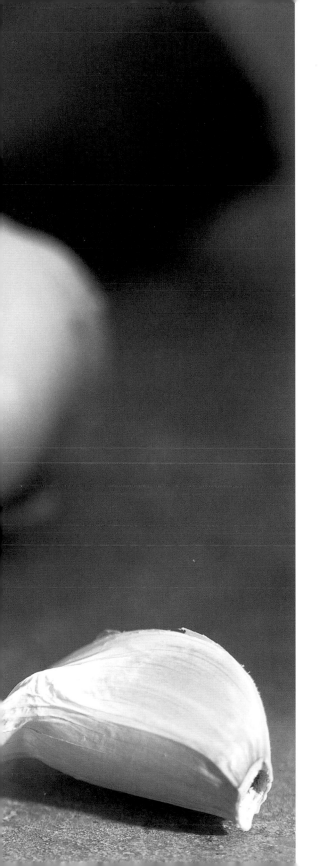

THE CLASSICS

From chicken soup with rice to Cajun gumbo, the recipes in this section are for classic soups and stews that you can always count on to satisfy your guests and yourself. These crowd-pleasers come from a variety of countries, but they are the gold standard of warming dishes to begin a meal or to serve as meals in themselves.

CHICKEN AND RICE SOUP

In a saucepan over high heat, bring the stock to a simmer. Reduce the heat to medium and add the chicken. Simmer until the chicken is just cooked through, about 2 minutes. Using a slotted spoon, transfer to a bowl and set aside.

Add the rice, onion, carrots, tomato, and mint to the hot stock, return to a simmer, and cook until the vegetables and rice are tender yet firm, about 15 minutes.

Add the zucchini and reserved chicken to the soup and simmer until the zucchini is tender, 3–4 minutes longer. Discard the mint sprigs. Season to taste with salt and pepper.

Ladle the soup into warmed bowls and serve at once.

MAKES 4–6 SERVINGS

RICE VARIETIES

Long-grain rice has elongated, slender grains that are much longer than they are wide. When cooked, the grains remain fluffy and separate, making them popular for pilafs and soups, such as in this recipe. Short-grain rice varieties tend to clump up and stick together when cooked, and are preferred for Asian and Caribbean cooking. Arborio and Carnaroli are Italian rices whose high starch contents make them perfect for risotto; jasmine rice is a perfumed rice popular in Thailand; and basmati rice, an aromatic, nutty rice, is used in Indian cooking.

6 cups (48 fl oz/1.5 l) chicken stock (page 112) or prepared broth

½ lb (250 g) boneless, skinless chicken breasts, cut into ½-inch (12-mm) dice

¼ cup (2 oz/60 g) long-grain white rice

1 yellow onion, finely chopped

2 carrots, peeled, halved lengthwise, and thinly sliced

1 tomato, peeled (page 109) and diced

4 sprigs fresh mint

1 zucchini (courgette), halved lengthwise and thinly sliced

Salt and freshly ground pepper

MANHATTAN CLAM CHOWDER

4 slices thick-cut bacon, cut into ½-inch (12-mm) dice

2 leeks, white and light green parts only, cleaned *(far right)* and finely chopped

3 stalks celery, cut into slices ½ inch (12 mm) thick

2 russet potatoes, peeled and cut into ½-inch (12-mm) dice

2 cloves garlic, minced

One 28-oz (875-g) can diced tomatoes, with juice

Two 6½-oz (200-g) cans minced clams, juice drained and reserved (see Note)

Salt and freshly ground pepper

2 teaspoons fresh lemon juice

2 tablespoons finely chopped fresh flat-leaf (Italian) parsley

Chowder crackers for serving (optional)

In a soup pot over medium-high heat, sauté the bacon until browned but not crisp, about 3 minutes. Add the leeks, celery, and potatoes and cook, stirring occasionally, until the vegetables are softened and nicely coated, about 3 minutes. Add the garlic and sauté for 1 minute longer. Add the tomatoes with their juice, 3 cups (24 fl oz/750 ml) water, and the reserved clam juice and bring to a boil over high heat. Reduce the heat to medium-low and simmer, covered, until the potatoes are tender when pierced with a fork, about 15 minutes.

Remove from the heat. Using a handheld or standing blender, coarsely purée the soup, making sure to leave some texture. Add the clams, salt and pepper to taste, and lemon juice and return to medium-low heat. Cook gently until the clams are heated through, about 3 minutes. Taste and adjust the seasoning. Add the parsley and stir to combine.

Ladle the chowder into warmed bowls and serve at once, topped with the crackers, if desired.

Note: Canned clams work well here because the clam juice gives the soup extra flavor. The minced clams are added at the last minute so that they stay tender.

MAKES 4–6 SERVINGS

CLEANING LEEKS

Leeks grow best in sandy soil, which means their tightly layered leaves often hide streaks of mud and grit. To clean leeks, cut off the roots at the base, trim off the tough, dark-green leaf tops, and peel off any bruised or discolored outer leaves from the stalk. Halve the leeks lengthwise (or cut into quarters if they are particularly large) and wash thoroughly under cold running water, gently spreading the leaves apart to rinse out any hidden grit or dirt.

VEGETARIAN CHILI

Place the beans in a bowl with cold water to cover and soak for at least 4 hours, or up to overnight. Drain and set aside.

In a Dutch oven over medium heat, heat the oil. Add the onions and sauté until softened, about 5 minutes. Add the garlic, oregano, cumin, coriander, paprika, cayenne, and chili powder and stir to combine. Cook, stirring so the mixture cooks evenly to release the flavors, about 3 minutes.

Add the tomatoes with their juice, chile to taste, the stock, and the drained beans and bring to a boil. Reduce the heat to low and cook, partially covered, until the beans are tender yet firm, 1–1½ hours. (If the mixture seems too thick, add a little water.) When the beans are tender, add the vinegar and cook for 1 minute longer. Add the chopped cilantro and stir to combine. Season to taste with salt.

To serve, ladle the chili into warmed bowls and serve at once.

Serving Tip: To add color and flavor, garnish each bowl of chili with shredded Cheddar cheese, sour cream, salsa, crumbled tortilla chips, and a sprig of cilantro.

Variation: If you like meat in your chili, sauté 1 lb (500 g) of ground (minced) turkey or beef until nicely browned and add to the chili with the cilantro.

MAKES 6–8 SERVINGS

CILANTRO

Used extensively in Mexican, Asian, and Latin American cuisines, this fresh green herb has a distinctive, slightly soapy flavor and a pungent scent. Cilantro looks like flat-leaf parsley, but with softer, more rounded leaves and finer stems. Also known as Chinese parsley or fresh coriander, it loses its pungency quickly when cooked, so add it at the end of cooking or use it raw. Cilantro wilts and yellows quickly, so don't buy it more than a day or two before you plan to use it.

2 cups (14 oz/440 g) dried pinto beans, picked over, rinsed, and drained

3 tablespoons canola oil

2 yellow onions, finely chopped

5 cloves garlic, minced

1 tablespoon plus 1 teaspoon *each* dried oregano and ground cumin

1 teaspoon ground coriander

1 tablespoon paprika

¼ teaspoon cayenne pepper

¼ cup (1 oz/30 g) high-quality chili powder

1½ cups (12 oz/375 g) canned diced tomatoes

½–1 canned *chile chipotle en adobo* (page 114), minced

5 cups (40 fl oz/1.25 l) vegetable stock (page 112)

1 tablespoon balsamic vinegar

3 tablespoons finely chopped fresh cilantro (fresh coriander), plus whole sprigs for garnish

Salt

FISHERMAN'S STEW WITH ROASTED GARLIC AIOLI

½ cup (4 fl oz/125 ml) mayonnaise (page 113)

2 tablespoons Roasted Garlic Purée *(far right)*

1 tablespoon lemon juice

1 pinch cayenne pepper

Salt and ground white pepper

2 tablespoons olive oil

2 leeks, white and light green parts only, cleaned (page 13) and thinly sliced

1 carrot, peeled and finely chopped

1 fennel bulb, trimmed and finely chopped

3 cloves garlic, minced

2 cups (16 fl oz/500 ml) fish stock (page 113) or bottled clam juice

2 cups (16 fl oz/500 ml) dry white wine

One 28-oz (875-g) can diced tomatoes, with juice

1 pinch saffron threads

Ground black pepper

2 lb (1 kg) white fish such as halibut or monkfish, cut into 1½-inch (4-cm) pieces

Finely chopped fresh chives for garnish

In a small bowl, combine the mayonnaise, garlic purée, lemon juice, cayenne, and salt and freshly ground white pepper to taste and mix well to combine. Taste and adjust the seasoning. Refrigerate until ready to use.

In a large Dutch oven over medium heat, heat the oil. Add the leeks, carrot, and fennel and sauté until softened, about 5 minutes. Add the garlic and sauté for 1 minute longer. Add the stock, wine, tomatoes with their juice, saffron, and salt and pepper to taste and bring to a simmer. Reduce the heat to medium-low, cover partially, and simmer until the vegetables are tender, about 20 minutes. Taste and adjust the seasoning. Remove from the heat. Using a handheld or standing blender, coarsely purée the soup, making sure to leave some texture.

Return the pot to medium heat. Add the fish pieces and cook until the fish is opaque throughout, 6–8 minutes. Taste and adjust the seasoning.

Ladle the stew into warmed deep bowls and top each serving with a spoonful of the aioli. Garnish with the chopped chives and serve immediately.

MAKES 4–6 SERVINGS

ROASTED GARLIC PURÉE
Roasting garlic turns its harsh bite into a mellow, earthy sweetness. Preheat the oven to 425°F (200°C). Using a small, sharp knife, cut off the top of each garlic head, exposing the cloves. Place the heads in a small roasting pan, drizzle with olive oil, and sprinkle with salt. Cover the pan tightly with aluminum foil and roast until the garlic is very soft when pierced with a knife, about 45 minutes. Remove from the oven and let cool briefly. Squeeze the soft garlic cloves out of their skins and mash with a fork or in a food processor to make a smooth purée.

BOEUF BOURGUIGNON

Preheat the oven to 350°F (180°C). In a frying pan over medium-high heat, sauté the bacon until browned but not crisp, about 3 minutes. Transfer to paper towels.

Pat the meat dry and season with salt and pepper. In a Dutch oven over medium-high heat, heat the oil. Working in batches to avoid crowding, add the beef and brown on all sides, 4–5 minutes per batch. Transfer the browned meat to a bowl and set aside.

Add the chopped onions and carrots to the pot and sauté over medium-high heat until the onions are lightly browned, about 4 minutes. Reduce the heat to low, sprinkle the flour on top, and cook, stirring, until the flour is incorporated, 1–2 minutes. Return the bacon and meat, along with any juices, to the pot.

Remove from the heat, add the Cognac, and flambé (page 21). Return to medium-low heat add the wine, stock, tomato paste, garlic, bay leaf, and salt and pepper to taste. Bring to a simmer. Transfer to the oven and braise, covered, until the meat is fork-tender and the stew is the consistency of thick cream, about 2 hours. Discard the bay leaf.

Meanwhile, in a frying pan over medium-high heat, melt 2 tablespoons of the butter. Add the mushrooms and sauté until browned, about 5 minutes. Transfer to a bowl. Melt the remaining 1 tablespoon butter, add the pearl onions, and cook, stirring, until lightly browned, about 5 minutes. Add ½ cup (4 fl oz/125 ml) water, cover, and cook until the onions are softened, 3–5 minutes. Transfer to the bowl with the mushrooms.

When ready to serve, stir the mushrooms, pearl onions, and 1 tablespoon of the parsley into the stew. Season to taste with salt and pepper. Transfer to a serving dish and garnish with the remaining 2 tablespoons parsley. Serve immediately.

MAKES 6 SERVINGS

PEARL ONIONS

Sweeter and less sharp-tasting than full-sized onions, pearl onions are no more than 1 inch (2.5 cm) in diameter, with papery skins. Because they hold their color and shape well when cooked, they make an attractive visual contrast in a deep-brown stew or braise. To remove the skins, trim off the root ends and blanch the onions in a saucepan of boiling water for 4 minutes. Drain, then quickly transfer them to a bowl of cold water to stop the cooking. Drain again and peel off the loosened skins; they should fall away easily.

6 strips bacon, cut into ½-inch (12-mm) pieces

3 lb (1.5 kg) beef chuck, cut into 1½-inch (4½-cm) cubes

Salt and ground pepper

2 tablespoons olive oil

2 yellow onions, finely chopped

2 carrots, peeled and finely chopped

3 tablespoons all-purpose (plain) flour

¼ cup (2 fl oz/60 ml) Cognac or other brandy

3 cups (24 fl oz/750 ml) dry, full-bodied red wine

1½ cups (12 fl oz/375 ml) beef stock (page 112)

1 tablespoon tomato paste

4 cloves garlic, minced

1 bay leaf

3 tablespoons butter

1 lb (500 g) white button mushrooms, quartered

7 oz (220 g) fresh pearl onions, blanched and peeled *(far left),* or frozen pearl onions, thawed

3 tablespoons finely chopped fresh flat-leaf (Italian) parsley

COQ AU VIN

6 strips thick-cut bacon, cut into 1-inch (2.5-cm) pieces

3½ lb (1.75 kg) chicken pieces such as breast halves, thighs, and legs

¼ cup (1½ oz/45 g) all-purpose (plain) flour

Salt and freshly ground pepper

3 tablespoons olive oil

¼ cup (2 fl oz/60 ml) Cognac or other brandy

2 cups (16 fl oz/500 ml) full-bodied dry red wine

1 tablespoon tomato paste

3 cloves garlic, minced

½ lb (250 g) white button mushrooms, brushed clean and cut into quarters

10 oz (315 g) fresh pearl onions, blanched and peeled (page 18), or frozen pearl onions, thawed

2 tablespoons finely chopped fresh flat-leaf (Italian) parsley

In a large Dutch oven over medium-high heat, sauté the bacon until crisp, 4–5 minutes. Transfer to paper towels to drain. Pour off all but 1 tablespoon of the drippings from the pot.

Pat the chicken dry with paper towels. Place the flour in a large bowl or lock-top plastic bag and season to taste with salt and pepper. Add the chicken in batches and stir or shake to coat thoroughly with the seasoned flour.

Add 2 tablespoons of the olive oil to the pot with the bacon drippings and heat over medium-high heat. Working in batches to avoid overcrowding, add the chicken and brown on all sides, 5–7 minutes for each batch. Transfer each browned batch to a bowl.

Return all the chicken and any accumulated juices to the pot. Remove from the heat, add the Cognac, and flambé *(right)*. Return to medium heat and stir in the wine, tomato paste, and garlic. Braise, covered, until the chicken is cooked through and the juices run clear when a thigh is pierced with a fork, about 50 minutes, turning the chicken once with tongs after 25 minutes.

Meanwhile, in a frying pan over medium heat, heat the remaining 1 tablespoon olive oil. Add the mushrooms and sauté until softened, 3–5 minutes. Raise the heat to medium-high and add the pearl onions. Cook, stirring, until the onions are lightly glazed and heated through, 3–5 minutes longer. Season to taste with salt and pepper.

When the chicken is done and the sauce is slightly thickened, add the reserved bacon, the mushroom mixture, and the parsley and stir to combine. Taste and adjust the seasoning. Transfer to a serving platter and serve immediately.

MAKES 4–6 SERVINGS

FLAMBÉING

Flambéing—pouring liquor over a dish and igniting it— is an essential step in many French dishes. To flambé safely, remove the pot from the heat before adding any liquor. Briefly return the pot to the heat to warm the liquor, and remove from the heat once more. Make sure flammable objects are moved away, and use a long kitchen match. Once lit, hold the match just above the liquor in the pan (you are lighting the fumes). The flame should burn out in 30 seconds. Keep a pot lid nearby to cover the pan if the flames don't subside within a minute.

GUMBO

FILÉ POWDER
Also known as gumbo filé, this olive-green powder is made from dried, pulverized leaves of the sassafras plant and is prized by the Cajuns of Louisiana for its thickening abilities. Its name comes from the French verb *filer*, which means "to spin threads," and true to its name, it can get stringy if cooked too long. Instead, add it just a few minutes before serving. Look for it in the spice aisle of well-stocked supermarkets, or try a specialty market that carries Southern food products.

In a large, heavy soup pot over medium heat, heat 2 tablespoons of the oil. Add the okra and sauté, stirring occasionally, until golden brown and softened, 12–15 minutes. Using a slotted spoon, transfer to a bowl and set aside.

Add 2 more tablespoons of the oil and heat over medium-high heat. Add the chicken and sauté until lightly browned on all sides, 3–5 minutes. Using a slotted spoon, transfer to another bowl and set aside.

Add the remaining 6 tablespoons (3 fl oz/90 ml) oil and heat for 2 minutes. Add the flour and stir until incorporated, to make a roux (page 109). Cook the roux, stirring constantly with a wooden spoon, until dark brown, about 4 minutes. Reduce the heat to medium, add the onions and bell peppers, and cook, stirring occasionally, until softened, 8–10 minutes. Add the garlic and cook 1 minute longer.

Add the cooked okra, tomatoes and juice, stock, bay leaves, Cajun seasoning, and salt and pepper to taste. Bring to a boil, then reduce the heat to low and simmer until slightly thickened, about 20 minutes. Add the browned chicken and cook until the chicken is cooked through, about 10 minutes longer.

Add the sausage and shrimp and cook until the sausage is heated through and the shrimp is evenly pink, about 3 minutes. Add the filé powder and cook 1 minute longer to allow the flavors to blend. Discard the bay leaves. Taste and adjust the seasoning, and serve at once in warmed bowls.

Serving Tip: Serve the gumbo on a bed of steamed white rice, garnished with parsley. Pass hot-pepper sauce at the table.

MAKES 6 SERVINGS

10 tablespoons (5 fl oz/ 160 ml) canola oil

½ lb (250 g) okra, trimmed and cut crosswise into ½-inch (12-mm) slices

2 lb (1 kg) skinless, boneless chicken thighs, cut into 2-inch (5-cm) pieces

6 tablespoons (2 oz/60 g) all-purpose (plain) flour

1 large yellow onion, chopped

1 *each* red and green bell pepper (capsicum), seeded and diced

3 cloves garlic, minced

One 14½-oz (455-g) can diced tomatoes, with juice

5 cups (40 fl oz/1.25 l) chicken stock (page 112)

2 bay leaves

2½–3 tablespoons Cajun seasoning blend (page 114)

Salt and freshly ground pepper

½ lb (250 g) andouille sausage, thickly sliced

1 lb (500 g) large raw shrimp (prawns), peeled and deveined (page 53)

1 teaspoon filé powder *(far left)*

SIMPLE SOUPS

Nothing is more satisfying than a quick, simple soup. It feeds all the senses, from the visual delight of a vivid green asparagus soup, to the fragrance of fresh-cooked vegetables in Mexican-style corn chowder. Served with salad and crusty bread, these recipes are perfect for a weeknight dinner or quick meal anytime.

CREAM OF ASPARAGUS SOUP

In a soup pot over medium heat, melt the butter with the olive oil. Add the leeks and sauté until softened, about 5 minutes. Add the asparagus pieces and potato and sauté until nicely coated and beginning to soften, about 3 minutes longer. Add the stock and salt and white pepper to taste. Bring to a boil over medium-high heat. Reduce the heat to low, cover partially, and cook until the vegetables are very tender, about 15 minutes.

While the soup is cooking, bring a small saucepan of water to a boil. Add the lemon juice and reserved asparagus tips and boil until they are crisp-tender and still bright green, about 3 minutes. Drain and set aside.

When the vegetables are tender, remove the soup from the heat. Using a handheld or standing blender, purée the soup until smooth. Taste and adjust the seasoning.

Ladle the soup into warmed bowls and garnish with a dollop of crème fraîche, some of the asparagus tips, and a sprinkling of the chives. Serve immediately.

Note: You can also make this same basic soup with other vegetables such as carrots or broccoli.

MAKES 4–6 SERVINGS

PEELING ASPARAGUS
Unless you've purchased slender springtime asparagus, you will need to trim asparagus spears of their woody ends and peel their skins before cooking. To find the point where the spear becomes tender, gently bend the stalk about 2 inches (5 cm) from the end. The stalk should snap naturally, right at the point where the tender and tough parts meet.
Using a vegetable peeler, scrape the thin outer layer of peel from an inch or two below the tip's leaf buds to the end of the stalk.

1 tablespoon unsalted butter

2 tablespoons olive oil

2 leeks, white and light green parts only, cleaned (page 13) and finely chopped

1 lb (500 g) asparagus, trimmed, peeled *(far left)*, and cut into 2-inch (5-cm) pieces, tips reserved

1 russet potato, peeled and cut into 2-inch (5-cm) chunks

4 cups (32 fl oz/1 l) chicken stock (page 112) or prepared broth

Salt and freshly ground white pepper

Juice of ½ lemon

3 tablespoons crème fraîche (page 103)

1 tablespoon finely chopped fresh chives

CHEDDAR CHEESE SOUP WITH ALE

½ cup (4 oz/125 g) unsalted butter

1 leek, white and light green part only, cleaned (page 13) and thinly sliced

1 carrot, peeled and cut into ½-inch (12-mm) dice

1 stalk celery, cut into ½-inch (12-mm) dice

Salt and freshly ground pepper

½ cup (2½ oz/75 g) all-purpose (plain) flour

½ teaspoon dry mustard

4 cups (32 oz/1 l) chicken stock (page 112) or prepared broth

1 bottle (12 oz/375 ml) good-quality ale such as Bass or Newcastle, poured into a bowl

2 cups (8 oz/250 g) shredded sharp Cheddar cheese (see Note)

¼ cup (1 oz/30 g) freshly grated Parmesan cheese

1 pinch cayenne pepper

1 teaspoon Worcestershire sauce

2 tablespoons finely chopped fresh flat-leaf (Italian) parsley

In a large saucepan over medium heat, melt the butter. Add the leek, carrot, and celery and sauté until softened, about 10 minutes. Season with salt and pepper.

Stir in the flour and mustard until incorporated and cook for about 1 minute. Add the stock and ale and bring to a simmer over high heat. Reduce the heat to medium and cook, whisking to break up any lumps of flour, until the mixture is slightly thickened, about 5 minutes. Add the cheeses and whisk constantly until nicely melted, 3–5 minutes longer. Do not let boil. Stir in the cayenne and Worcestershire sauce. Taste and adjust the seasoning.

Ladle the soup into warmed bowls, garnish with the parsley, and serve immediately, garnished with additional cheese or garlic toasts (page 113).

Note: This savory soup was inspired by Welsh rabbit (a classic supper dish of melted sharp cheese sauce poured over toast). You can try different types of Cheddar cheese from America, Canada, or Ireland to make this recipe. Make sure not to boil the soup after adding the cheese, or the soup may develop a stringy texture.

MAKES 4–6 SERVINGS

ALE

Ale is the staple pub drink of Great Britain. Compared to mild American-style lagers, ales have a heavier body and a more assertive taste due to being fermented at a warmer temperature. Ales are also generally higher in alcohol, usually between 5 and 8 percent by volume as opposed to 4 percent for an average lager.

MEXICAN CORN CHOWDER

In a soup pot over medium heat, melt the butter with the olive oil. Add the onion and sauté until softened, about 5 minutes. Add the bell pepper and sauté until slightly softened, about 3 minutes longer. Add 2¼ cups (13½ oz/425 g) of the corn kernels and cook for about 3 minutes. Add the stock and jalapeños to taste and bring to a boil. Reduce the heat to low and simmer slowly, partially covered, until the vegetables are very soft, about 20 minutes.

Meanwhile, bring a small saucepan of water to a boil. Add the remaining ¼ cup (1½ oz/45 g) corn kernels and boil until crisp-tender, about 2 minutes. Drain and set aside.

When the vegetables are soft, remove from the heat. Using a handheld or standing blender, coarsely purée the soup, making sure to leave some texture. Add the cream and salt and white pepper to taste, and reheat gently over low heat. Taste and adjust the seasoning.

Ladle the soup into warmed bowls, garnish with the blanched corn and the cilantro, and serve immediately.

MAKES 6 SERVINGS

CUTTING CORN OFF THE COB

Fresh corn in season has a sweet, creamy flavor that is unmatched by canned or frozen corn. To cut corn kernels off the cob, cut the stem end flush with the base of the ear. Stand the cob on the stem end in a shallow bowl. Using a sharp knife, slice down, cutting off the tender part of the kernels but leaving the sharp base of the kernels attached to the cob. Rotate the cob after each cut until you have detached all the kernels. Run the back of the knife down over the empty cob to squeeze out the sweet corn "milk."

2 tablespoons unsalted butter

3 tablespoons olive oil

1 large yellow onion, coarsely chopped

1 large red bell pepper (capsicum), seeded and coarsely chopped

2½ cups (15 oz/470 g) corn kernels, from about 5 ears of corn *(far left)*

6 cups (48 fl oz/1.5 l) chicken stock (page 112) or prepared broth

1–2 jalapeño chiles, seeded (page 65) and finely chopped

½ cup (4 fl oz/125 ml) heavy (double) cream

Salt and freshly ground white pepper

2 tablespoons chopped fresh cilantro (fresh coriander)

CHICKEN AND VEGETABLE STRACCIATELLA

5 cups (40 fl oz/1.25 l) chicken stock (page 112) or prepared broth

3 cloves garlic, thinly sliced

1 small carrot, peeled and julienned *(far right)*

1 small stalk celery, julienned *(far right)*

2 tablespoons freshly grated Parmesan cheese

4 tablespoons (⅓ oz/10 g) finely chopped fresh flat-leaf (Italian) parsley

1 lb (500 g) skinless, boneless chicken breasts, cut into slices ½ inch (12 mm) thick

½ lb (250 g) spinach leaves, cut into very thin strips

2 eggs, lightly beaten

Salt and freshly ground pepper

In a saucepan, combine the stock and garlic and bring to a boil over medium-high heat. Add the carrot and celery, cover, and cook until the vegetables are just tender, about 4 minutes.

Add the cheese, 2 tablespoons of the parsley, the chicken, and spinach. Return to a simmer and cook until the chicken is just cooked through, the spinach is wilted but still bright green, and the cheese is melted, about 2 minutes. Remove from the heat.

Pour the eggs into the soup. Stir back and forth with a fork until white threads of cooked egg appear. Season to taste with salt and pepper. Ladle into warmed bowls and garnish with the remaining 2 tablespoons of parsley. Serve immediately.

Note: Stracciatella *means "little rag," and that's what the eggs resemble once added to the soup. Simple and economical, this is Italy's version of egg-drop soup.*

Safety Tip: This dish contains eggs that may be only partially cooked. For more information, see page 114.

MAKES 4 SERVINGS

JULIENNING

To julienne a vegetable means to cut it into thin, narrow strips of equal size. Cut this way, hard vegetables such as carrots and celery cook quickly and evenly, and their neat appearance adds a pleasingly professional look to the dish. To julienne carrots and celery stalks, using a sharp chef's knife or a mandoline, first trim off the rounded edges, cutting the vegetables into square-sided logs. Cut crosswise into 2-inch (5-cm) pieces, then cut each piece lengthwise into slices ⅛ inch (3 mm) thick. Stack the slices and cut lengthwise into thin strips.

SUMMER SQUASH AND LEEK PURÉE

In a soup pot over medium heat, heat the olive oil. Add the leeks and sauté until softened, about 5 minutes. Add the squash and sauté until lightly browned, about 5 minutes longer. Add the garlic and cook for 1 minute longer.

Add the stock and cook, partially covered, until the squash is very tender, about 15 minutes. Remove from the heat. Using a handheld or standing blender, purée the soup until smooth. Stir in the basil, the 2 tablespoons chives, the milk, and the lemon juice. Season to taste with salt and pepper. Reheat gently over medium-low heat.

Ladle the soup into warmed bowls and garnish with chives. Serve immediately.

MAKES 4–6 SERVINGS

3 tablespoons olive oil

2 leeks, white and light green parts only, cleaned (page 13) and finely chopped

6 yellow crookneck squash, about 1½ lb (750 g) total weight, thinly sliced

2 cloves garlic, minced

4 cups (32 fl oz/1 l) chicken stock (page 112) or prepared broth

3 tablespoons finely chopped fresh basil

2 tablespoons finely chopped fresh chives, plus extra for garnish

1 cup (8 fl oz/250 ml) whole milk

2 teaspoons fresh lemon juice

Salt and freshly ground pepper

SUMMER SQUASH
Summer squash are the thin-skinned, warm-weather cousins to winter's pumpkins and acorn squashes. Dark-green zucchini (courgettes) and yellow summer (crookneck) squash are the most common types, but farmers' markets often stock a wide variety, including round, scallop-edged green or white pattypans; round, deep yellow sunburst; and green, tennis-ball-sized Ronde de Nice squashes. Look for firm squash no more than 8 inches (20 cm) long; larger ones tend to have large seeds and watery, bitter flesh.

CELERY ROOT–POTATO PURÉE

3 tablespoons unsalted
butter

2 leeks, white and light
green parts only, cleaned
(page 13) and coarsely
chopped

1 celery root (celeriac),
peeled and cut into
1-inch (2.5-cm) dice

2 russet potatoes, peeled
and coarsely chopped

6 cups (48 fl oz/1.5 l)
chicken or vegetable
stock (page 112) or
prepared broth

Salt and freshly ground
white pepper

1 tablespoon white
truffle oil

Finely chopped fresh
flat-leaf (Italian) parsley
for garnish (optional)

In a soup pot over medium heat, melt the butter. Add the leeks and sauté until softened, 4–5 minutes. Add the celery root and potatoes and sauté until slightly softened, about 5 minutes.

Add the stock and bring to a simmer. Cover partially and cook until the vegetables are very soft, about 20 minutes. Remove from the heat. Using a handheld or standing blender, purée the soup until smooth. Season to taste with salt and white pepper. Reheat gently over medium-low heat.

Ladle the soup into warmed bowls, drizzle with truffle oil, and garnish with the parsley, if using. Serve immediately.

MAKES 6 SERVINGS

CELERY ROOT

Large, knobby celery root (celeriac) might look a bit alien, but under the thick, rough skin is a versatile vegetable with a mild, celery-like flavor. To prepare celery root, trim off the bottom and any remaining stalks at the top. Scrub well with a stiff brush under cold running water. Using a small, sharp knife or vegetable peeler, remove the brownish skin, including any deep grooves of embedded soil; cut as directed. If not using right away, place cut pieces in a bowl of cold water with 1–2 teaspoons of lemon juice to prevent darkening.

SHRIMP AND SNOW PEA SOUP

Place the noodles in a bowl with hot water to cover and let soak until very pliable, about 15 minutes. Drain and set aside.

In a soup pot, combine the stock, ginger, half the sliced green onions, the mirin, sesame oil, and soy sauce. Bring to a boil over high heat. Add the shrimp, drained noodles, snow peas, and mushrooms and cook until the shrimp are slightly opaque throughout and the mushrooms are heated through, about 2 minutes. Add the cornstarch mixture and cook until slightly thickened, about 1 minute longer. Season to taste with salt and pepper.

Ladle the soup into warmed bowls and garnish with the remaining sliced green onion.

MAKES 4–6 SERVINGS

ENOKI MUSHROOMS
These white Japanese mushrooms still grow in the wild, but the cultivated species has become widely available. Growing in clusters with long slender stems and small, gumdrop-shaped caps, they have a striking appearance and a delicate flavor. Look for them in Asian markets, sold fresh, canned, or packed in water in plastic tubs.

3½ oz (105 g) cellophane noodles (page 114)

6 cups (48 fl oz/1.5 l) chicken stock (page 112) or prepared broth

2 teaspoons peeled and minced fresh ginger

2 green (spring) onions, including tender green parts, thinly sliced

2 tablespoons mirin or other rice wine

1 teaspoon dark sesame oil

2 teaspoons soy sauce

1 pound (500 g) large shrimp (prawns), peeled and deveined (page 53)

¼ lb (125 g) snow peas (mangetouts), trimmed and cut in half crosswise

¼ lb (125 g) enoki mushrooms (far left), brushed clean and stems trimmed

2 teaspoons cornstarch (cornflour) mixed with 2 tablespoons water

Salt and freshly ground pepper

FIRST-COURSE
SOUPS

In this chapter you'll find starters for a wide range of dinners, from wonton soup for an Asian-inspired menu to a spicy tortilla soup to start off a festive dinner party. And the seasons are considered here as well, with cool vichyssoise and fresh pea soup with mint for summer, and a bisque made with winter squash and apples to begin a winter meal.

VICHYSSOISE WITH WATERCRESS

In a soup pot over medium heat, heat the olive oil. Add the leeks and sauté until softened, about 4 minutes. Add the potatoes and sauté until softened, about 5 minutes longer. Add the watercress and sauté until wilted but still bright green, about 3 minutes. Add the stock and bring to a simmer. Cover partially and cook until the vegetables are very tender, about 15 minutes.

Remove from the heat. Using a handheld or standing blender, purée the soup until smooth. Transfer to a bowl and season to taste with salt and white pepper. Stir in the cream and lemon juice. Cover and refrigerate until well chilled, at least 4 hours or up to overnight. (You may also reheat it gently and serve it hot, but this soup is traditionally served cold.)

Combine the lemon zest and chives in a small bowl. Mix thoroughly. Ladle the soup into chilled serving bowls and garnish with the zest mixture.

MAKES 6–8 SERVINGS

WHITE PEPPER

White and black peppercorns start off as the same berry on the tropical pepper vine. Black peppercorns are harvested slightly underripe and dried with their skins on, while white peppercorns are allowed to fully ripen, then are boiled to remove the dark hulls. Most of the peppercorn's heat is concentrated in the hull, so white pepper has a milder flavor than black. Because of their pale color, white peppercorns are preferred for seasoning light-colored dishes such as this soup.

3 tablespoons olive oil

4 leeks, white and light green parts only, cleaned (page 13) and coarsely chopped

1½ lb (750 g) white or red potatoes, peeled and coarsely chopped

Leaves of 1 bunch watercress

8 cups (64 fl oz/2 l) chicken stock (page 112) or prepared broth

Salt and freshly ground white pepper

1 cup (8 fl oz/250 ml) heavy (double) cream

1 tablespoon fresh lemon juice

Grated zest of 1 lemon

1 tablespoon finely chopped fresh chives

CHILLED BEET BORSCHT WITH DILL CREAM

8 beets, about 2 lb (1 kg) total weight, scrubbed and trimmed (far right)

1 yellow onion, cut into quarters

8 cups (64 fl oz/2 l) chicken stock (page 112) or prepared broth

1 tablespoon sugar

2 cucumbers, peeled, seeded (page 110), and julienned

4 tablespoons (⅓ oz/10 g) finely chopped fresh dill

2 tablespoons fresh lemon juice

2 tablespoons unseasoned rice wine vinegar

Salt and freshly ground black pepper

1 cup (8 oz/250 g) sour cream

Freshly ground white pepper

In a large nonaluminum soup pot, combine the beets, onion quarters, stock, sugar, and 1 cup (8 fl oz/250 ml) water. Cover and bring to a boil over medium-high heat. Reduce the heat to low and simmer, still covered, until the beets are tender when pierced with the tip of a knife, 30–35 minutes.

With a slotted spoon, transfer the beets to a bowl and let cool. Reserve the cooking liquid. When cool enough to handle, peel the beets under cool running water. Cut the beets in half crosswise. Reserve 6 beet halves. Cut the remaining beets into julienne (page 33). Cover and refrigerate until ready to use.

Strain the reserved cooking liquid through a fine-mesh sieve into a large bowl. Discard the onions. In a blender or food processor, combine the reserved beet halves with 1 cup (8 fl oz/250 ml) of the sbeet cooking liquid and process to a smooth purée. Add to the bowl with the remaining cooking liquid. Cover and refrigerate until well chilled, at least 4 hours, or preferably overnight.

When ready to serve, add the julienned beets and cucumbers, 2 tablespoons of the dill, the lemon juice, vinegar, and salt and black pepper to taste to the soup. Mix well until incorporated. Taste and adjust the seasoning.

In a small bowl, combine the sour cream, the remaining 2 tablespoons dill, and salt and white pepper to taste, and mix well.

Ladle the soup into chilled bowls and garnish with the dill cream.

MAKES 8 SERVINGS

PREPARING BEETS
The rich magenta hue of beets is beautiful on the table but tricky in the kitchen, where it can dye everything from fingernails to cutting boards. To prepare beets, scrub them thoroughly and trim the stems to ½ inch (12 mm), leaving the skin and root "tail" intact (so the beets' flavorful juices won't escape during cooking). If you wish, wear kitchen gloves and cover the cutting board with plastic wrap to prevent staining.

SPRING PEA SOUP WITH FRESH MINT

In a large saucepan over medium heat, heat the olive oil. Add the chopped whites of the onions and the carrot and sauté until softened, 3–5 minutes. Add the lettuce and sauté until wilted, about 5 minutes longer.

Add 3 tablespoons of the mint, the stock, and the shelled peas if using. Bring to a simmer, cover, and cook until the vegetables are tender, about 20 minutes. If using thawed frozen peas, add during the last 5 minutes.

Remove from the heat. Using a handheld or standing blender, purée the soup until smooth. Add the cream, lemon juice, and salt and white pepper to taste. Reheat gently over medium-low heat for about 5 minutes. Taste and adjust the seasoning.

Ladle the soup into warmed bowls and garnish with 1 tablespoon sour cream, a little of the remaining 1 tablespoon mint, and the chopped greens of the onions.

Note: This versatile soup tastes equally good hot or cold. If you are going to serve it cold, refrigerate it for at least 4 hours, or up to overnight.

MAKES 4–6 SERVINGS

FRESH PEAS

English, or green, peas are the familiar spring and early summer peas, which must be shelled before cooking. Try to taste a pea before buying, if possible; they should taste sweet rather than starchy or chalky. The season for fresh peas is short, but frozen peas— in particular *petits pois*, usually labeled "petite" or "baby" peas—are a respectable alternative, as they retain their flavor much better than most frozen vegetables.

2 tablespoons olive oil

6 green (spring) onions, white parts only, finely chopped, plus finely chopped green parts for garnish

1 large carrot, peeled and finely diced

1 small head butter (Boston) lettuce, cored and cut into shreds

4 tablespoons (⅓ oz/10 g) chopped fresh mint

4 cups (32 fl oz/1 l) chicken stock (page 112) or prepared broth

2 cups (10 oz/315 g) shelled English peas (about 2 lb/1 kg in the pod) or thawed frozen *petits pois* (far left)

¼ cup (2 fl oz/60 ml) heavy (double) cream or half-and-half (half cream)

1 tablespoon fresh lemon juice

Salt and freshly ground white pepper

4–6 tablespoons (2–3 oz/ 60–90 g) sour cream

CREAM OF TOMATO SOUP WITH A PESTO SWIRL

¼ cup (2 fl oz/60 ml) olive oil

1 yellow onion, finely chopped

1 carrot, peeled and finely chopped

1 stalk celery, finely chopped

1 clove garlic, minced

¼ cup (1½ oz/45 g) all-purpose (plain) flour

6 tomatoes, peeled, seeded (page 109), and coarsely chopped, or one 28-oz (875-ml) can diced tomatoes with juice

2 tablespoons chopped fresh basil leaves

¼ cup (2 oz/60 g) tomato paste

1 teaspoon sugar

3 cups (24 fl oz/750 ml) chicken or vegetable stock (page 112) or prepared broth

1 cup (8 fl oz/250 ml) whole milk

Salt and freshly ground white pepper

4–6 tablespoons (2–3 oz/ 60–90 g) basil pesto, homemade (page 113) or purchased (optional)

In a large saucepan over medium heat, heat the olive oil. Add the onion and sauté until translucent, about 3 minutes. Add the carrot and celery and sauté until the vegetables are softened, about 5 minutes longer. Add the garlic and sauté for 1 minute longer.

Reduce the heat to low. Sprinkle the flour over the vegetables and cook, stirring constantly, until the flour is incorporated and the mixture is thickened, 1–2 minutes.

Add the tomatoes, basil, tomato paste, sugar, and stock and bring to a simmer over medium-high heat. Reduce the heat to medium and cook, partially covered, stirring occasionally, until all of the vegetables are tender and the flavors are well blended, about 20 minutes. Remove from the heat. Using a handheld or standing blender, coarsely purée the soup, making sure to leave some texture. Stir in the milk and reheat gently over medium-low heat. (Do not allow the soup to boil or it may separate.) Season to taste with salt and white pepper.

Ladle the soup into warmed bowls and swirl 1 tablespoon of pesto, if using, into each. Serve immediately.

MAKES 4–6 SERVINGS

TOMATO VARIETIES

Although heirloom tomatoes, in a riot of colors and picturesque shapes, have become a common sight in the tomato section of many markets during their season, traditional dense-fleshed plum (Roma) tomatoes or small round red tomatoes such as Early Girl are still the best for making sauces and soups. Store tomatoes at room temperature, stem side down, for up to 3 days.

WINTER SQUASH AND APPLE BISQUE

In a soup pot over medium-high heat, melt the butter. Sauté the onion and shallots until softened, about 5 minutes. Add the apples and squash and cook until nicely coated, about 3 minutes longer. Add the stock and rosemary and bring to a simmer. Add the thyme. Reduce the heat to medium and simmer, covered, until the vegetables are very tender, about 25 minutes.

Remove from the heat. Using a handheld or standing blender, purée the soup until smooth. Stir in the half-and-half and season with salt and pepper. Reheat gently over medium-low heat.

Ladle the soup into warmed bowls and garnish with the sour cream and rosemary and thyme leaves.

MAKES 6–8 SERVINGS

WINTER SQUASH

Hard-shelled winter squash come in brilliant autumn colors and fanciful shapes. For this soup, you can substitute another dense, richly flavored orange squash, such as a turban, or one of the small pumpkins meant for cooking, such as Sugar Pie or Baby Bear, for the butternut. To peel and seed winter squash, using a large, sharp knife, carefully halve the squash lengthwise. Scoop out the strings and seeds and discard. Using a sharp vegetable peeler or a paring knife, peel away the tough skin, along with any green spots under the peel.

2 tablespoons unsalted butter

1 large yellow onion, finely chopped

2 shallots, finely chopped

2 pippin, Granny Smith, or other tart apples, peeled, cored, and cut into 2-inch (5-cm) chunks

1 butternut squash, about 2 lb (1 kg), peeled, seeded, and cut into 2-inch (5-cm) chunks *(far left)*

6 cups (48 fl oz/1.5 l) chicken stock (page 112) or prepared broth

1 teaspoon finely chopped fresh rosemary, plus whole leaves for garnish

2 teaspoons finely chopped fresh thyme, plus whole leaves for garnish

½ cup (4 fl oz/125 ml) half-and-half (half cream)

Salt and freshly ground pepper

½ cup (4 fl oz/125 ml) sour cream

WONTON SOUP

FOR THE FILLING:

¼ lb (125 g) shrimp (prawns), shelled, deveined *(far right)*, and finely chopped

¼ lb (125 g) ground (minced) pork or turkey

3 canned water chestnuts, finely chopped

3 green (spring) onions, including tender green parts, finely chopped

1 clove garlic, minced

1 teaspoon peeled and minced fresh ginger

1 teaspoon soy sauce

½ teaspoon sesame oil

1 pinch sugar

Salt and freshly ground white pepper

About 24 wonton skins (see Note)

Cornstarch (cornflour)

6 cups (48 fl oz/1.5 l) chicken stock (page 112) or prepared broth

½ teaspoon sesame oil

¼ lb (125 g) baby spinach leaves

2 green (spring) onions, including tender green parts, sliced

To make the filling, in a bowl, combine the shrimp, pork, water chestnuts, green onions, garlic, ginger, soy sauce, sesame oil, sugar, and salt and white pepper to taste. Mix well. To test the seasoning, heat a dry nonstick frying pan over medium-high heat, add 1 teaspoon of the filling, and cook until the meat and shrimp are cooked through, about 2 minutes. Taste for seasoning, and adjust the remaining filling as necessary.

Lay out the wonton skins on a lightly floured work surface. Sprinkle a baking sheet with cornstarch, and have a small bowl of water nearby. Spoon 1 scant teaspoonful of the raw filling in the center of each wonton skin. Dip your finger in the water and moisten 2 perpendicular edges of 1 wonton skin. Fold it in half to make a triangle, with the 2 moistened edges meeting the 2 dry edges. Press the edges to seal them well, and press gently around the filling. Then moisten the 2 opposite points of the long side of the wonton and press them together to form a little "cap" or bag. Place the completed wonton on the prepared baking sheet. Repeat with the remaining wontons.

Bring a large pot three-fourths full of water to a boil over high heat. Working in batches, carefully add the wontons, cover, and return to a boil. Cook the wontons until they are al dente, 3–4 minutes longer. Using a strainer, carefully transfer to a bowl.

Meanwhile, combine the stock and sesame oil in a large saucepan and bring to a boil over medium-high heat. Add the spinach leaves and simmer until the spinach is wilted but still bright green, about 2 minutes.

Divide the cooked wontons among warmed bowls. Ladle over the hot broth and garnish with the green onions. Serve immediately.

Note: Wonton skins are available at Asian markets.

MAKES 4–6 SERVINGS

CLEANING SHRIMP

To clean shrimp (prawns), first cut off the head (if still attached), then pull off the legs inside the curl of the body. Peel off the shell, beginning at the head end. Using a small, sharp knife, cut a shallow central groove along the back of the shrimp. With the tip of the knife, lift out the thin black vein of the shrimp's intestinal tract and discard. Rinse the shrimp under cold running water.

TORTILLA SOUP WITH VEGETABLES

In a soup pot over medium heat, heat the oil. Add the onion and sauté until golden brown, about 7 minutes; do not burn. Add the garlic and 2 tablespoons of the cilantro and sauté 1 minute longer. Add the tomatoes with their juice and the cumin and cook, stirring occasionally, until slightly thickened, about 5 minutes. Stir in the stock and remove from the heat. Using a handheld or standing blender, purée the soup until smooth.

Return the soup to medium-low heat. Add the zucchini and carrot, partially cover, and cook, stirring occasionally, until the vegetables are tender, about 15 minutes. Season to taste with salt and pepper.

Meanwhile, preheat the oven to 400°F (200°C). Arrange the tortilla strips in a single layer on a baking sheet and bake until crisp and beginning to brown, 7–8 minutes. Set aside.

Place the chile in a dry cast-iron or nonstick frying pan over medium-high heat and cook until it is fragrant and puffed, about 2 minutes per side; do not let burn. Remove the stem, crush the chile in a mortar or with the side of a heavy knife, and set aside.

Ladle the soup into warmed bowls. Garnish with the toasted tortilla strips, crushed chile, remaining 2 tablespoons cilantro, and cheese. Serve immediately.

MAKES 4 SERVINGS

2 tablespoons corn or canola oil

1 yellow onion, finely chopped

4 cloves garlic, minced

4 tablespoons (⅓ oz/10 g) chopped fresh cilantro (fresh coriander)

One 14½-oz (455-g) can diced fire-roasted tomatoes (page 115), with juice

1 teaspoon ground cumin

4 cups (32 fl oz/1 l) vegetable or chicken stock (page 112) or prepared broth

1 zucchini (courgette), julienned (page 33)

1 carrot, peeled and julienned (page 33)

Salt and freshly ground pepper

4 corn tortillas, slightly stale or dry, halved crosswise and sliced into thin strips

1 dried pasilla chile, stemmed and seeded

¼ cup (1 oz/30 g) coarsely shredded Monterey jack cheese

MAIN-COURSE SOUPS

When combined with a green salad and good bread, these hearty soups make wholesome and nourishing meals in a bowl. Combining meat, seafood, or beans with vegetables and a wide variety of seasonings and spices, these filling dishes appeal most when the weather turns chilly.

SPLIT PEA SOUP WITH ANDOUILLE SAUSAGE
58

CREAMY MUSHROOM SOUP WITH VELVET CHICKEN
61

RIBOLLITA
62

POZOLE
65

FISH CHOWDER WITH WHITE WINE AND CREAM
66

VIETNAMESE BEEF AND NOODLE SOUP
69

PORTUGUESE KALE AND SAUSAGE SOUP
70

SPLIT PEA SOUP WITH ANDOUILLE SAUSAGE

ANDOUILLE SAUSAGE

Andouille sausage adds a bit of Cajun spice to this soup, which is more commonly made with ham or bacon. A rustic, cooked smoked sausage stuffed with tripe, andouille originated in France but is a treasured ingredient in Louisiana's Cajun country, where it is a staple ingredient in gumbo and jambalaya. Cooked sausages such as andouille can be stored in the refrigerator for up to 1 week or frozen for up to 2 months.

In a large Dutch oven over medium heat, heat the olive oil. Add the onion and sauté until softened, 3–5 minutes. Add the celery and carrots and sauté until softened, 2–3 minutes longer. Add the garlic and sauté for 1 minute longer.

Add the split peas, ½ cup (4 oz/125 g) of the diced sausage, the stock, bay leaf, and 4 cups (32 fl oz/1 l) water and bring to a simmer over medium-high heat. Reduce the heat to medium-low, cover partially, and cook, stirring occasionally and scraping the bottom of the pot so the peas do not scorch, until the peas are tender, about 45 minutes.

Remove from the heat and discard the bay leaf. Using a handheld or standing blender, coarsely purée the soup, making sure to leave some texture. Return to medium-low heat, add the remaining sausage, and cook until the sausage is heated through, about 5 minutes. Season to taste with salt and pepper.

Ladle the soup into warmed bowls and garnish with the parsley. Serve immediately.

MAKES 8 SERVINGS

2 tablespoons olive oil

1 large yellow onion, finely chopped

2 stalks celery, thinly sliced

3 carrots, peeled and thinly sliced

3 cloves garlic, minced

2 cups (14 oz/440 g) yellow split peas, picked over, rinsed, and drained

½ lb (250 g) andouille sausage, cut into ½-inch (12-mm) dice

4 cups (32 fl oz/1 l) chicken stock (page 112) or prepared broth

1 bay leaf

Salt and freshly ground pepper

Finely chopped fresh flat-leaf (Italian) parsley for garnish

CREAMY MUSHROOM SOUP WITH VELVET CHICKEN

1 oz (30 g) dried mush-rooms such as porcini

4 cups (32 fl oz/1 l) chicken stock (page 112) or prepared broth

¼ cup (2 oz/60 g) unsalted butter

1 yellow onion, finely chopped

¾ lb (375 g) fresh cremini mushrooms, brushed clean and thinly sliced (far right)

¼ cup (1½ oz/45 g) all-purpose (plain) flour

Salt and freshly ground white pepper

2 teaspoons soy sauce

1 lb (500 g) skinless, boneless chicken breasts, halved lengthwise and cut into thin slices

1 cup (8 fl oz/250 ml) half-and-half (half cream)

¼ cup (2 fl oz/60 ml) tawny Port

Finely chopped fresh flat-leaf (Italian) parsley for garnish

In a saucepan, combine the dried mushrooms and stock. Cover, bring to a boil over medium-high heat, and cook, simmering, for 5 minutes. Remove from the heat and set aside.

In a large soup pot over medium heat, melt the butter. Add the onion and sauté until softened, about 5 minutes. Add the fresh mushrooms and sauté until softened, about 3 minutes longer. Sprinkle the onion mixture with the flour and salt and white pepper to taste and cook, stirring, until the flour is incorporated and the mushrooms are coated, about 1 minute. Drain the soaked dried mushrooms through a colander lined with damp cheesecloth (muslin), reserving the stock. Add the stock, drained mushrooms, and the soy sauce to the same pot and simmer, partially covered, until the mushrooms are tender and the flavors have married, about 15 minutes.

Remove from the heat. Using a handheld or standing blender, coarsely purée the soup, making sure to leave some texture. Return to medium heat, add the chicken, and simmer until just cooked through, about 2 minutes. Add the half-and-half and Port and simmer until the flavors are blended, about 1 minute longer. Taste and adjust the seasoning as desired.

Ladle the soup into warmed bowls, garnish with the chopped parsley, and serve immediately.

MAKES 4 SERVINGS

CLEANING MUSHROOMS
Mushrooms absorb water easily, becoming soggy and flavorless if left to soak. Generally, store-bought fresh mushrooms need only to be rubbed with a soft brush or clean cloth, but if the mush-rooms seem very dirty, rinse the loose dirt away quickly in a colander. Another effective technique is to gently rub the mushrooms with a damp paper towel.

RIBOLLITA

Place the beans in a bowl with cold water to cover and soak for at least 4 hours, or up to overnight. Drain and set aside.

In a large soup pot, combine the drained beans, 3 qt (3 l) of water, the garlic, and the sage. Bring to a boil over medium-high heat. Reduce the heat to low and simmer until the beans are tender yet firm, 1½–2 hours. Remove from the heat. Using a handheld or standing blender, coarsely purée the beans, making sure to leave some texture. Set aside.

In a large saucepan over medium heat, heat ¼ cup (2 fl oz/60 ml) of the olive oil. Add the onions and sauté until softened, 7–10 minutes. Add the carrots, celery, potatoes, savoy cabbage, chard, and cavolo nero. Toss to coat them evenly. Add the tomatoes and salt and pepper to taste. Cover and cook, stirring occasionally, until the greens are tender, about 20 minutes.

Add the cooked vegetables to the puréed beans and cook, covered, until nicely thickened, about 40 minutes longer. Taste and adjust the seasoning.

Place the toasted bread slices at the bottom of warmed bowls and ladle the soup on top; drizzle with the remaining olive oil, and serve immediately.

Note: Also known as black cabbage, Tuscan cavolo nero is very similar to dinosaur kale, also called lacinato kale. If cavolo nero is not available, dinosaur or regular kale makes a fine substitute.

Serving Tip: Ribollita, whose name means "reboiled" in Italian, can be served the day it is made, but it is even better when reheated and eaten the next day, after the flavors have melded (hence the name).

MAKES 8 SERVINGS

BREAD FOR RIBOLLITA

A staple of Tuscan peasant cooking, this soup is traditionally made with stale bread; like French toast or *panzanella* (bread and tomato salad), this is a clever way of using up leftovers instead of letting them go to waste. In Tuscany, the bread would be *pane toscano*, distinctive for its lack of salt, but a crusty country-style loaf will do. You can use stale bread if you have it on hand, or you can lightly toast fresh bread as a substitute. Either way, the dry bread will soak up plenty of flavorful soup.

1 lb (500 g) dried cannellini beans, picked over, rinsed, and drained

4 cloves garlic, chopped

5 fresh sage leaves

½ cup (4 fl oz/125 ml) extra-virgin olive oil

2 yellow onions, coarsely chopped

3 carrots, peeled and coarsely chopped

3 stalks celery, sliced

2 russet potatoes, peeled and coarsely chopped

½ small savoy cabbage, cored and coarsely chopped

1 bunch *each* Swiss chard and cavolo nero (see Note), thick ribs removed, coarsely chopped

One 14½-oz (455-g) can crushed tomatoes

Salt and freshly ground pepper

8 slices stale or toasted country-style bread, about ½ inch (12 mm) thick

POZOLE

2 tablespoons corn
or canola oil

1 lb (500 g) pork tender-
loin, cut into ½-inch
(12-mm) dice

1 yellow onion, finely
chopped

3 cloves garlic, minced

1½ tablespoons chili
powder

½ teaspoon ground cumin

½ teaspoon dried oregano

3 cups (24 fl oz/750 ml)
chicken stock (page 112)
or prepared broth

One 14½-oz (455-g)
can diced fire-roasted
tomatoes (page 115),
with juice

One 15-oz (470-g) can
white hominy, rinsed
and drained (see Note)

1 jalapeño chile, seeded
and diced (far right)

Salt and freshly ground
pepper

Avocado slices and sliced
green (spring) onions
for garnish

Lime wedges and warm
tortillas for serving

In a soup pot over medium heat, heat the oil. Working in batches
if necessary to avoid overcrowding the pan, add the pork and
sauté until opaque on all sides but not browned, about 3 minutes
per batch. Using a slotted spoon, transfer the meat to a bowl
and set aside.

Add the onion to the pot and sauté until softened, 3–5 minutes.
Add the garlic, chili powder, cumin, and oregano and cook,
stirring to blend the spices evenly, for 1 minute longer.

Add the stock, tomatoes, hominy, jalapeño, sautéed pork with any
juices, and salt and pepper to taste, and bring to a boil over high
heat. Reduce the heat to low, cover, and simmer until the pork is
cooked through and the soup is fragrant, about 15 minutes.

Ladle the soup into warmed bowls and garnish with the avocado
slices and green onions; serve with the lime wedges and warm
tortillas alongside.

*Note: Pozole also means hominy, or maize. Traditionally made
with partially cooked hominy* (nixtamal), *this easier version of this
Mexican soup uses drained and rinsed canned white hominy.*

MAKES 4 SERVINGS

WORKING WITH CHILES

Capsaicin, the chemical that
gives chiles their heat, is
found mostly in the cottony
ribs and membranes inside the
pepper's pod. The seeds, flesh,
and skin have progressively
less heat, so if you want to cut
down on the firepower of a
chile, remove the membranes
and seeds before using. When
working with chiles, avoid
touching your eyes, mouth,
nose, or other sensitive areas.
You may wish to wear rubber
gloves to protect your skin.
Wash your hands and utensils
immediately after working
with chiles.

FISH CHOWDER WITH WHITE WINE AND CREAM

In a frying pan over medium heat, melt 2 tablespoons of the butter. Add the leeks and sauté until softened, about 5 minutes. Add the mushrooms and sauté until just beginning to soften, about 3 minutes. Add the bell pepper and sauté until beginning to soften, about 2 minutes longer. Set aside.

In a large soup pot, combine the stock and wine and bring to a boil over medium-high heat. Cook until reduced to about 4 cups (32 fl oz/1 l), about 10 minutes. Add the cream, return to a slow simmer, and cook until just thickened, about 10 minutes longer. Add the saffron and salt and white pepper to taste.

Add the fish, return to a simmer, and cook until the fish is tender, moist, and opaque throughout, 3–5 minutes. Add the sautéed vegetables, stir to combine, and cook gently until heated through, about 3 minutes more.

Ladle the soup into warmed bowls, garnish with the chopped parsley, and serve immediately.

MAKES 6 SERVINGS

SAFFRON

Renowned for its earthy, slightly bitter flavor, the vivid brick-red threads of saffron are the hand-plucked stigmas of a type of crocus flower. As each crocus has only three stigmas, harvesting saffron is enormously time-consuming, making saffron the world's most expensive spice. But it takes only a pinch of saffron to add a brilliant yellow tint and subtle flavor to a pot of soup or a pan of Spanish paella. For best results, use saffron threads, not powder.

3 tablespoons unsalted butter

3 leeks, white and light green parts only, cleaned (page 13) and finely chopped

¼ lb (125 g) white mushrooms, brushed clean and sliced

1 red bell pepper (capsicum), seeded and julienned (page 33)

4 cups (32 fl oz/1 l) fish stock (page 113) or bottled clam juice

1 cup (8 fl oz/250 ml) dry white wine

1 cup (8 fl oz/250 ml) heavy (double) cream

Generous pinch of saffron threads *(far left)*

Salt and freshly ground white pepper

1½ lb (750 g) firm-fleshed white fish fillets such as sea bass or halibut, cut into bite-sized chunks

Finely chopped fresh flat-leaf (Italian) parsley for garnish

VIETNAMESE BEEF AND NOODLE SOUP

7 oz (220 g) rice stick noodles (page 115)

8 cups (64 fl oz/2 l) beef stock (page 112)

5 whole cloves

4 thin slices fresh ginger

3 star anise pods

1 cinnamon stick

1 teaspoon black peppercorns

1 yellow onion, sliced

Salt and ground pepper

¼ cup (2 fl oz/60 ml) peanut or canola oil

8 shallots, sliced

½ lb (250 g) eye of round beef, very thinly sliced by the butcher, cut into 2-inch (5-cm) pieces

Leaves of 1 bunch fresh cilantro (fresh coriander)

Leaves of 1 bunch *each* fresh mint and basil, preferably Thai basil

1 cup (2 oz/60 g) bean sprouts

2 small red Thai chiles, seeded and thinly sliced

1 lime, cut into quarters

Hot sauce, such as Sriracha, for serving

In a bowl, combine the rice sticks with warm water to cover and let soak until very pliable, about 20 minutes.

Meanwhile, in a soup pot, combine the stock, cloves, ginger, star anise, cinnamon, peppercorns, onion, and salt and pepper to taste. Bring to a boil over medium-high heat. Reduce the heat to low, cover, and cook until the broth is fragrant, about 10 minutes. Strain the soup into a large bowl through a fine-mesh sieve, discarding the spices. Return the stock to the pot, and set aside.

While the stock is simmering and the noodles are softening, heat the oil in a frying pan over medium-high heat. Add the shallot slices and fry, turning them with tongs, until evenly browned on both sides, about 4 minutes. Transfer to paper towels to drain.

Have ready 4 large, deep soup bowls. Bring a large pot of water to a boil over high heat. Reheat the seasoned beef broth to a boil over high heat. Drain the noodles. Place one-fourth of the noodles in a strainer and immerse in the boiling water until tender yet firm, about 10 seconds. Drain and place in one of the soup bowls. Repeat with the remaining noodles and the other bowls.

Divide the beef slices among the bowls, then ladle over the boiling broth (the hot broth will cook the thin beef slices). Divide the cilantro, mint, basil, bean sprouts, chiles, fried shallots, and lime wedges among the bowls.

Serve immediately, passing the hot sauce at the table.

MAKES 4 SERVINGS

PHO

Pho, pronounced "fuh," is a popular Vietnamese noodle soup that many consider to be the national dish. The base is a strong beef broth perfumed with star anise, peppercorns, and ginger. Translucent rice noodles float in the wide bowl, topped by a choice of meats, from tripe and tendon to thinly sliced steak. *Pho* is always accompanied by sprigs of fresh Thai basil, mint, and cilantro, along with a plate of mung bean sprouts, wedges of lime, and sliced chiles.

PORTUGUESE KALE AND SAUSAGE SOUP

In a large soup pot over medium heat, heat the olive oil. Add the onions and sauté until lightly browned, 5–7 minutes. Add the garlic and cook for 1 minute longer. Add the potatoes, toss to coat, and sauté for 2 minutes longer. Add the stock, cover, and bring to a boil. Reduce the heat to a simmer and cook until the potatoes are tender, about 20 minutes.

Remove from the heat. Using a handheld or standing blender, coarsely purée the soup, making sure to leave some slices of potato intact. Add the sausage, cover, return to medium heat, and simmer until the sausage is heated through, about 5 minutes. Add the kale and cook, uncovered, until it is wilted but still bright green, 3–5 minutes. Season to taste with salt and pepper.

Ladle the soup into warmed bowls, drizzle with extra-virgin olive oil, and serve immediately.

MAKES 4–6 SERVINGS

CALDO VERDE

This soup, called *caldo verde*, or "green broth," is a signature dish for Portuguese communities in the United States. Kale, a staple of Portuguese cooking and the centerpiece of this hearty soup, is high in vitamins and easy to grow during the cool winter months. In Portugal, the sausage used would be linguiça or chorizo, but any garlicky pork sausage, such as kielbasa, will do. *Caldo verde* is often served with a golden hunk of *broa*, a yeasted cornbread, but southern-style quick cornbread makes a fine accompaniment.

¼ cup (2 fl oz/60 ml) olive oil

2 yellow onions, finely chopped

4 cloves garlic, minced

3 large russet potatoes, about 2½ lb (1.25 kg) total weight, peeled and thinly sliced

6 cups (48 fl oz/1.5 l) chicken or vegetable stock (page 112) or prepared broth

¾ lb (375 g) kielbasa or other cooked sausage, cut into slices ½ inch (12 mm) thick

1 bunch kale, thick stems and ribs removed, thinly sliced

Salt and freshly ground pepper

Extra-virgin olive oil for drizzling

HEARTY STEWS

Dishes such as paprika-rich goulash or a rich white bean stew may be quintessential winter fare, but stew can also star at a spring or summer meal, as in the case of bouillabaisse or tangy orange-scented lamb stew. Simply put, the recipes in this chapter are perfect any time you want a comforting one-pot meal.

BOUILLABAISSE

Remove any pin bones from the fish fillets. Cut the fillets crosswise into pieces 1½ inches (4 cm) wide. Set aside.

In a soup pot over medium-high heat, heat 2 tablespoons of the olive oil. Add the onions and carrot, reduce the heat to medium, and cook, stirring frequently, until the onions are soft and starting to turn golden, about 6 minutes. Add the garlic, leeks, and fennel and cook until the fennel is soft, 5 minutes. Add the tomatoes and orange and lemon zests and cook for 10 minutes longer. Add the bouquet garni and the fish stock. Raise the heat to high and bring to a boil. Add the remaining 2 tablespoons olive oil and continue cooking at a rapid boil until the flavors have melded, 15 minutes.

Reduce the heat to medium and add the fish fillets, shrimp, and mussels, discarding any that do not close to the touch. Cook until the mussels start to open, about 3 minutes longer. Discard any mussels that have not opened. Season with salt and pepper.

Ladle the soup into warmed serving bowls. Spread the toasted baguette slices with rouille and use to garnish the soup, or serve them alongside.

Note: This famous fish soup is a signature dish of Marseilles, in the south of France. In Marseilles, bouillabaisse broth is traditionally strained and served first with croutons and rouille (left). The shrimp, fish, and mussels are then served as a second course.

MAKES 6–8 SERVINGS

ROUILLE

To make rouille, cook 1 peeled, quartered russet potato in a saucepan of boiling water until tender, 15 minutes. Drain and chop. In a frying pan over medium heat, heat ¼ cup (2 fl oz/60 ml) olive oil. Add 4 halved cloves garlic and sauté until golden, 1 minute. Transfer the garlic and oil to a food processor. Add 2 coarsely chopped roasted red bell peppers (page 114), the potato, ¼ cup (2 fl oz/ 60 ml) water, 1 tablespoon fresh lemon juice, and 2 pinches of cayenne. Process until smooth. Season with salt and pepper.

1½ lb (750 g) mixed firm fish fillets such as striped bass, halibut, or monkfish

¼ cup (2 fl oz/60 ml) olive oil

3 yellow onions, chopped

1 carrot, peeled and grated

8 cloves garlic, minced

2 leeks, including tender green parts, chopped

1 fennel bulb, trimmed and cut into small dice

4 tomatoes, peeled, seeded (page 109), and chopped

Zests of 1 orange and 1 lemon, removed in wide ribbons with a peeler

1 bouquet garni (page 99)

8 cups (64 fl oz/2 l) fish stock (page 113)

¾ lb (375 g) shrimp, peeled and deveined (page 53)

1 lb (500 g) mussels, scrubbed and debearded (page 110)

Salt and freshly ground pepper

1 baguette, cut into thin slices and lightly toasted

Rouille for serving *(far left)*

ROASTED VEGETABLE STEW WITH COUSCOUS

8 carrots, peeled

1 eggplant (aubergine), peeled

4 yellow crookneck squash

2 leeks, white and light green parts only, cleaned (page 13) and finely chopped

½ lb (250 g) baby brussels sprouts, halved

3 tablespoons olive oil

4 cups (32 fl oz/1 l) chicken or vegetable stock (page 112)

1 teaspoon finely chopped fresh thyme leaves

Salt and ground pepper

6 cloves garlic, minced

1 tomato, peeled (page 109) and diced

1 cup (5 oz/155 g) Kalamata olives

One 15-oz (470-g) can chickpeas (garbanzo beans), rinsed and drained

2 tablespoons *each* finely chopped fresh flat-leaf (Italian) parsley, fresh chives, and fresh basil

¼ cup (1 oz/30 g) freshly grated Parmesan cheese

1¼ cups (10 oz/315g) cooked couscous

Preheat the oven to 400°F (200°C).

Cut the carrots, eggplant, and squash into 1½-inch (4-cm) chunks. In a large roasting pan, combine the carrots, eggplant, squash, leeks, and brussels sprouts. Pour in the olive oil and 1 cup (8 oz/250 ml) of the stock. Add the thyme and salt and pepper to taste and mix well to coat all the vegetables evenly.

Roast for 30 minutes, stirring the vegetables occasionally. Add another 1 cup stock, the garlic, and tomato to the pan and continue roasting, stirring every 15 minutes, until the vegetables are very tender, about 30 minutes longer.

Pit and chop the Kalamata olives *(right)*. Add the remaining 2 cups stock, the chickpeas, olives, parsley, chives, and basil to the pan and stir to combine. Taste and adjust the seasoning, and return to the oven for 5 minutes more.

Spoon the vegetables into a large serving bowl, garnish with the cheese, and serve each portion on a bed of couscous.

MAKES 6 SERVINGS

PITTING OLIVES

Almond-shaped, purplish-black Kalamata olives from Greece have a full, briny flavor and a meaty texture. A cherry or olive pitter makes quick work of removing the pits. Otherwise, spread the olives in a single layer on a cutting board. Crush them gently with the bottom of a heavy pan, a rolling pin, or the side of a chef's knife. Most of the pits should roll out of the cracked olives; remove any remaining pits with a small, sharp knife.

WHITE BEAN AND SAUSAGE STEW

Place the beans in a bowl with cold water to cover and soak for at least 4 hours, or up to overnight. Drain and set aside.

In a Dutch oven over medium heat, heat the olive oil. Add the onion and sauté until softened, 5–7 minutes. Add the garlic and sauté for 1 minute longer. Add the stock, wine, tomatoes, and drained beans. Bring to a simmer, cover, and cook until the beans are tender and beginning to fall apart, about 1¼ hours. Mash some of the beans with a back of a spoon to create a creamy consistency. Add the sausage, return to a simmer, and cook until thickened slightly, about 5 minutes. Add the balsamic vinegar and salt and pepper to taste; cook for 3 minutes longer to mellow the vinegar flavor.

Preheat the broiler (grill). Transfer the stew to a flameproof baking dish or gratin dish.

In a small bowl, combine the Parmesan, bread crumbs, and parsley. Sprinkle evenly over the stew. Slip under the broiler and broil (grill) until the bread crumbs and cheese are browned but not burned, 3–4 minutes. Serve in warmed soup bowls.

Note: This hearty recipe is a quicker, easier take on the traditional French cassoulet.

MAKES 6 SERVINGS

BREAD CRUMBS

Fresh bread crumbs are a great way to use up one- or two-day-old bread. For toasted bread crumbs, as required here, gently toast bread slices in a 325°F (165°C) oven until dry and lightly browned, 10–12 minutes. Break the slices (including the crusts) into pieces and process in batches in a food processor or blender to the desired texture.

2 cups (14 oz/440 g) dried white beans such as Great Northern, picked over, rinsed, and drained

2 tablespoons olive oil

1 yellow onion, finely chopped

2 cloves garlic, minced

4 cups (32 fl oz/1 l) chicken stock (page 112) or prepared broth

1 cup (8 fl oz/250 ml) dry white wine

1 cup (8 oz/250 g) drained canned diced tomatoes

1 lb (500 g) cooked sausage (such as chicken herb, lamb, or garlic sausage), cut into ½-inch (12-mm) slices

3 tablespoons balsamic vinegar

Salt and freshly ground pepper

¼ cup (1 oz/30 g) freshly grated Parmesan cheese

¼ cup (1 oz/30 g) toasted bread crumbs *(far left)*

1 tablespoon finely chopped fresh flat-leaf (Italian) parsley

CHICKEN FRICASSEE WITH DUMPLINGS

3 lb (1.5 kg) chicken thighs, legs, and breasts

1½ cups (7½ oz/235 g) all-purpose (plain) flour

Salt and ground pepper

4 tablespoons (2 fl oz/ 60 ml) olive oil

4 leeks, white and light green parts only, cleaned (page 13) and thinly sliced

2 yellow onions, thinly sliced

6 carrots, peeled and sliced

4 stalks celery, sliced

2 red apples, peeled, cored, and sliced

3 tablespoons finely chopped fresh dill

3 cups (24 fl oz/750 ml) chicken stock (page 112)

1 cup (8 fl oz/250 ml) apple juice

⅓ cup (2 oz/60 g) cornmeal

2 teaspoons baking powder

3 tablespoons chilled vegetable shortening

½–1 cup (4–8 fl oz/ 250–500 ml) milk, as needed

Pat the chicken pieces dry with paper towels. Place ¼ cup (1½ oz/ 45 g) of the flour in a large bowl or lock-top plastic bag and season with salt and pepper. Add the chicken in batches and stir or shake to coat thoroughly with the seasoned flour.

In a large Dutch oven over medium-high heat, heat 3 tablespoons of the olive oil. Working in batches to avoid crowding, add the chicken and brown on all sides, 4–5 minutes per batch. Transfer the browned chicken to a bowl and set aside.

Add the remaining 1 tablespoon olive oil to the pot and reduce the heat to medium. Add the leeks and onion and sauté until lightly browned, 5–7 minutes. Add the carrots, celery, and apples and sauté until slightly softened, 3–5 minutes longer. Add 2 tablespoons of the dill, the stock, and the apple juice and bring to a simmer. Return the chicken and any accumulated juices to the pot and cook, covered, until the chicken is cooked through and the juices run clear when a thigh is pierced with a knife, about 15 minutes. Season with salt and pepper.

Meanwhile, make the dumplings: In a bowl, mix the remaining 1¼ cups (6½ oz/200 g) flour, the cornmeal, baking powder, ½ teaspoon salt, and the remaining 1 tablespoon dill. Using a pastry blender or 2 knives, cut in the shortening; add the milk, stirring with a fork until the dough holds together in a rough mass.

Using an ice cream scoop, scoop up spoonfuls of the dumpling batter and arrange over the chicken pieces in the simmering broth (you should have 6–8 dumplings). Cover and cook, spooning some of the broth over the dumplings once or twice, until a skewer inserted into a dumpling comes out clean, 15–18 minutes.

Ladle the stew into warmed bowls, dividing the chicken pieces and dumplings among them. Serve immediately.

MAKES 4–6 SERVINGS

DILL

This feathery green herb is used frequently in Eastern European and Russian cooking, where it adds its distinctive aroma to all kinds of dishes, from chicken soup and marinated herring to dill pickles (flavored with dill seeds) and beet borscht. Here, dill's refreshing flavor adds an extra dimension to fluffy dumplings in a dill-scented chicken stew.

GOULASH

In a large Dutch oven over medium-high heat, heat the olive oil. Add the leeks and caraway seeds and sauté until the leeks are softened, about 5 minutes. Add the bell pepper and sauté until softened, about 2 minutes longer.

Add the beef and paprika and sauté until the beef is evenly browned on all sides, 7–10 minutes.

Raise the heat to high, add the stock, and bring to a boil. Using a wooden spoon, scrape up the browned bits on the bottom of the pan. Reduce the heat to medium-low, cover partially, and simmer until the meat is fork-tender, 30–40 minutes.

Stir in the tomatoes and juice, garlic, potato, parsnip, carrots, and salt and pepper to taste. Cook, partially covered, until all the vegetables are tender, about 20 minutes longer. Stir in the parsley. Taste and adjust the seasoning.

Ladle the stew into warmed soup bowls and garnish with the sour cream. Serve immediately.

MAKES 4 SERVINGS

PAPRIKA
To give an authentic flavor to this savory stew, look for Hungarian sweet paprika in the spice section of well-stocked supermarkets or specialty-food stores. Unlike most mild American paprika, which adds little but color, this dark red powder has a rich, aromatic flavor that captures the essence of the dried and milled paprika peppers from which it is made. Hungarian paprika is produced in five grades based on piquancy and heat; the sweet type, called for in this recipe, is the most versatile and easiest to find.

3 tablespoons olive oil

4 leeks, white and light green parts only, cleaned (page 13) and finely chopped

2 teaspoons caraway seeds

1 red bell pepper (capsicum), seeded and chopped

2 lb (1 kg) stewing beef, cut into 1-inch (2.5-cm) cubes

3 tablespoons sweet Hungarian paprika *(far left)*

3 cups (24 fl oz/750 ml) chicken, beef, or vegetable stock (page 112)

One 14½-oz (455-g) can diced tomatoes, with juice

3 cloves garlic, minced

1 *each* Yukon gold potato and parsnip, peeled and chopped

2 carrots, peeled and chopped

Salt and freshly ground pepper

¼ cup finely chopped fresh flat-leaf (Italian) parsley

½ cup (4 oz/125 g) sour cream

WINTER BEEF AND VEGETABLE STEW

3 lb (1.5 kg) beef chuck, cut into 1½-inch (4-cm) cubes

½ cup (2½ oz/75 g) all-purpose (plain) flour

Salt and ground pepper

5 tablespoons (3 fl oz/ 80 ml) olive oil

¼ cup (2 fl oz/60 ml) red wine vinegar

2 yellow onions, 1 parsnip, and 1 carrot, peeled and sliced

2 cups (16 oz/500 ml) beef stock (page 112) or prepared broth

1 cup (8 fl oz/250 ml) dry red wine

¼ cup (2 oz/60 g) tomato paste

2 cloves garlic, minced

1 bay leaf

4 sprigs fresh flat-leaf (Italian) parsley, plus more, chopped, for garnish

1 sprig fresh sage or ½ teaspoon dried sage

¾ lb (375 g) tender young carrots, peeled

7 oz (220 g) fresh pearl onions, blanched and peeled (page 18)

Pat the beef dry with paper towels. Place the flour in a large bowl or lock-top plastic bag and season to taste with salt and pepper. Add the beef in batches and stir or shake to coat thoroughly with the seasoned flour.

In a large Dutch oven over medium-high heat, heat 4 tablespoons (2 fl oz/60 ml) of the olive oil. Working in batches, add the beef and brown it evenly on all sides, 5–7 minutes for each batch. Transfer to a bowl and set aside.

Add the vinegar to the pot and, using a wooden spoon, scrape up the browned bits on the bottom of the pan. Reduce the heat to medium and add the remaining 1 tablespoon olive oil to the pot. Add the onions and sauté until well browned, 12–15 minutes. Add the sliced parsnip and carrot and sauté until slightly tender, about 3 minutes longer. Add the stock, browned beef and any accumulated juices, wine, tomato paste, garlic, bay leaf, parsley sprigs, and sage, and stir to mix well.

Reduce the heat to low, cover, and simmer, stirring occasionally, until the meat is almost fork-tender, about 1½ hours.

Add the young carrots, return to a simmer, and cook until the carrots are tender, about 15 minutes. Add the pearl onions and cook until just heated through, about 3 minutes longer. Discard the bay leaf and sage sprigs, if using. Season to taste with salt and pepper. Ladle into warmed soup bowls and garnish with the chopped parsley. Serve immediately.

Note: If not eating the same day, let the stew cool slightly, refrigerate overnight, remove any excess fat, and gently reheat. The flavors will be wonderfully melded.

MAKES 6 SERVINGS

DEGLAZING

Deglazing is a classic French technique. After meat or poultry is browned in a sauté pan, the meat is removed and a liquid (usually stock or wine, but in this case, vinegar) is added to the pan and brought to a boil over high heat. As the liquid boils, scrape the bottom of the pan with a wooden spoon to dislodge any flavorful browned bits stuck to the bottom of the pan before adding the remaining ingredients. This quick step melds the pan's tasty residue into the finished dish.

MOROCCAN LAMB STEW

Preheat the oven to 350°F (180°C). In a Dutch oven over medium heat, heat 1 tablespoon of the olive oil. Add the onions and sauté until softened, about 5 minutes. Add the carrots and cook until slightly softened, about 3 minutes longer. Transfer to a bowl and set aside.

Pat the lamb dry with paper towels. Place the flour in a large bowl or lock-top plastic bag and season with salt and pepper. Add the lamb in batches and stir or shake to coat thoroughly with the seasoned flour.

Add the remaining 3 tablespoons oil to the pot and heat over medium-high heat. Working in batches to avoid crowding, add the lamb and brown on all sides, 4–5 minutes for each batch. Transfer to a bowl and set aside.

Return the onion mixture and browned lamb along with any accumulated juices to the pot. Add the garlic, cumin, saffron, and ginger and stir to coat the meat and vegetables. Add the stock and bring to boil, scraping up the browned bits on the bottom of the pan with a wooden spoon. Add the tomatoes, dates, and orange zest and juice and bring to a boil over high heat.

Cover and bake in the oven until the meat is tender, 1½–2 hours. (If the sauce seems too thin, transfer the meat and vegetables to a bowl with a slotted spoon and boil the sauce on the stove top until thickened. Return the meat and vegetables to the pot.) Taste and adjust the seasoning.

Transfer the stew to a serving bowl and garnish with the parsley. Serve immediately.

MAKES 6 SERVINGS

DRIED DATES

Many people assume that wrinkled, sticky dates are a dried fruit, much like prunes or dried apricots. In fact regular dates are fresh fruits that acquire many of the same characteristics as dried fruit—thin skin, extreme sweetness—because they are grown in the desert. In this recipe, we call for dried dates. You will find this specialty food sold chopped and often covered with flour to prevent sticking. They act as a perfect sweet foil to highly spiced lamb stews.

4 tablespoons (2 fl oz/ 60 ml) olive oil

2 yellow onions, finely chopped

3 carrots, peeled and chopped

3 lb (1.5 kg) cubed lamb for stewing

½ cup (2½ oz/75 g) all-purpose (plain) flour

Salt and freshly ground pepper

3 cloves garlic, minced

1 teaspoon ground cumin

¼ teaspoon saffron threads (page 66)

1 tablespoon peeled and minced fresh ginger

2½ cups (20 fl oz/625 ml) beef stock (page 112) or prepared broth

1 cup (8 oz/250 g) canned crushed tomatoes

1 cup (6 oz/185 g) chopped dried dates

Grated zest and juice of 1 orange

2 tablespoons finely chopped fresh flat-leaf (Italian) parsley

POT AU FEU

3 qt (3 l) chicken stock (page 112) or prepared broth

3½ lb (1.75 kg) first-cut beef brisket

4 beef shanks, ¾–1 lb (375–500 g) each, with marrow bone

9 small leeks, white and light green parts only, cleaned (page 13)

2 tablespoons black peppercorns

2 bay leaves

8 carrots, peeled and cut in half crosswise

8 baby red potatoes, scrubbed

Salt

Dijon mustard, horseradish cream (page 115), and French bread for serving

In a large soup pot, combine the stock, brisket, beef shanks, and 3 qt (3 l) water. The beef should be well covered with liquid. Slice one of the leeks, bundle it with the peppercorns and bay leaves in a piece of cheesecloth (muslin), and tie with kitchen string to make a bouquet garni (page 99). Add to the pot. Bring to a simmer over medium heat and cook, uncovered, for 20–30 minutes, using a slotted spoon or skimmer to skim off the foam that rises to the surface.

Partially cover the pot, reduce the heat to low, and simmer very gently until the meat is fork-tender, about 2½ hours. Skim occasionally to remove any foam. Using a fork and a slotted spoon, transfer the meat to a platter. Cover loosely with aluminum foil to keep warm.

Cut the remaining 8 leeks lengthwise down the middle but leave them intact at the base. Add the leeks, carrots, potatoes, and salt to taste to the pot. Return to a simmer over medium-low heat and cook gently until the vegetables are just tender, 20–30 minutes. Discard the bouquet garni. Taste and adjust the seasoning.

Using a slotted spoon, transfer the brisket and shank meat to a cutting board. Thinly slice the brisket against the grain and break up the shank meat into pieces. Divide the meat and vegetables among warmed bowls. Ladle over the broth and serve with thick slices of bread for dipping. Pass the Dijon mustard and horseradish cream at the table.

Note: Make sure you give yourself plenty of time to prepare this dish, since it can't be hurried. Pot au feu is traditionally served in two courses, first the broth and then the meat and vegetables. This version is simpler to serve and more informal. Provide diners with a knife and fork in addition to a soup spoon.

MAKES 8 SERVINGS

SHANK AND MARROW
The shank, or lower leg, is a naturally well exercised muscle on any animal. The meat is flavorful and succulent but requires long, slow cooking to tenderize it (the shank is also the main ingredient in osso buco). Marrow, considered by many to be a delicacy, is found at the center of the shank bone. After cooking pot au feu or similar dishes, it can be scooped out of the bone by diners and eaten spread on sliced French bread or alongside the meat.

BRAISES

Braises are the busy cook's best friend: they cook slowly, almost unattended, on the stove top or in a low oven until tender and imbued with rich, delicious flavor. They also have the virtue of improving with time; make these dishes one day ahead and reheat them the next day for an even greater depth of flavor.

CHICKEN CACCIATORE

Pat the chicken breasts dry with paper towels and season with salt and pepper. In a large frying pan over medium-high heat, heat 2 tablespoons of the olive oil. Working in batches if necessary to avoid overcrowding the pan, add the chicken and brown it on all sides, 4–5 minutes. Transfer to a bowl and set aside.

Add the remaining 2 tablespoons olive oil to the pan. Add the onions and sauté until softened and lightly browned, about 5 minutes. Add the mushrooms and bell peppers and sauté until slightly softened, 3–4 minutes longer. Add the garlic and cook for 1 minute longer.

Pour the red wine into the pan. Bring to a boil, scraping up the browned bits on the bottom of the pan with a wooden spoon. Add the tomatoes with their juice, tomato paste, parsley, basil, and oregano. Season to taste with salt and pepper. Reduce the heat to medium-low and simmer until the sauce is slightly thickened, about 10 minutes. Add the reserved chicken along with any accumulated juices, cover, and braise, simmering gently until the chicken is opaque throughout, about 20 minutes. Add the vinegar and the olives, if using, and cook until the olives are heated through, about 3 minutes. Taste and adjust the seasoning. Serve in warmed shallow bowls.

Serving Tip: Rice is the classic accompaniment with this braise.

MAKES 6 SERVINGS

BALSAMIC VINEGAR

The distinctive sweet-sour flavor of balsamic vinegar has become tremendously popular over the last few years. Traditional balsamic vinegar is made from *mosto cotto*, the cooked, concentrated juice of Italian Trebbiano grapes, aged in a succession of wooden barrels for many years until it becomes a rich and intense syrup. For cooking, a good-quality balsamic vinegar made from wine vinegar flavored with a small percentage of *mosto cotto* is perfectly acceptable.

6 chicken breast halves, skin on and bone in, about ½ lb (250 g) each

Salt and freshly ground pepper

4 tablespoons (2 fl oz/ 60 ml) olive oil

2 yellow onions, thinly sliced

1½ lb (750 g) white mushrooms, brushed clean and sliced

1 *each* red and yellow bell pepper (capsicum), seeded, deribbed, and thinly sliced

4 cloves garlic, minced

1½ cups (12 fl oz/375 ml) dry red wine

One 28-oz (875-g) can diced tomatoes, with juice

1 tablespoon tomato paste

3 tablespoons chopped fresh flat-leaf (Italian) parsley

1 teaspoon dried basil

1 teaspoon dried oregano

1 tablespoon balsamic vinegar

½ cup (2½ oz/75 g) pitted Kalamata olives (page 77), optional

BRAISED CHICKEN
WITH TOMATILLOS AND CILANTRO

3 Anaheim or poblano chiles (see Note)

3½ lb (1.75 kg) chicken pieces such as breast halves, thighs, and legs

4 tablespoons (2 fl oz/ 60 ml) vegetable oil

1 large yellow onion, finely chopped

2 cups (16 fl oz/500 ml) chicken stock (page 112) or prepared broth

6 cloves garlic, minced

1½ lb (750 g) tomatillos, husked and cut into quarters *(far right)*

3 tablespoons finely chopped fresh cilantro (fresh coriander), plus whole leaves for garnish

½ teaspoon ground cumin

1 tablespoon fresh lime juice

Salt and freshly ground pepper

Warm tortillas for serving

Preheat the broiler (grill). Place the chiles on a baking sheet about 6 inches (15 cm) from the heat source and broil (grill), using tongs to turn them, until blackened on all sides. Transfer to a paper bag, close tightly, and let stand 10 minutes. Peel the chiles, remove the stems, seeds, and ribs (page 65), and chop finely. Set aside.

Pat the chicken dry with paper towels. In a large frying pan over medium-high heat, heat 2 tablespoons of the oil. Working in batches to avoid crowding, add the chicken and brown it on all sides, 4–5 minutes. Transfer to a bowl and set aside.

Reduce the heat to medium and add the remaining 2 tablespoons oil. Add the onion and sauté until softened, 3–5 minutes. Stir in the chicken stock, scraping the browned bits from the bottom of the pan with a wooden spoon.

Add the garlic, roasted chiles, tomatillos, chopped cilantro, and cumin. Bring to a boil, then reduce the heat to low. Return the chicken and any accumulated juices to the pan and simmer, covered, turning once, until the chicken pieces are just cooked through and the juices run clear when a thigh is pierced with a knife, about 20 minutes. (The smaller pieces will be done first.) Transfer the chicken to a platter and tent with aluminum foil.

Add the lime juice to the pan and cook the sauce over high heat until slightly reduced and thickened. Season to taste with salt and pepper. Pour the sauce over the chicken pieces and garnish with the cilantro leaves. Serve with the warm tortillas.

Note: For a mild dish, use Anaheim chiles; for a hotter version, use poblanos. If you are unable to find fresh chiles, the canned variety will do.

MAKES 6 SERVINGS

TOMATILLOS

Small, round, and green, tomatillos look like unripe cherry tomatoes—they're even known as *tomates verdes* in Mexico. (Both tomatoes and tomatillos are members of the nightshade family.) Tomatillos have a tart herbal taste and can be used in *salsa verde*, soups, and stews. To remove the husks, hold the fruit under warm running water, strip off the husk, and rinse off the sticky residue coating the skin.

QUICK-BRAISED PORK CHOPS
WITH CIDER AND DRIED FRUIT

QUICK BRAISES

Braising is a two-part process. First, the meat is quickly browned to give it a good color and add flavor to the sauce. Then a small amount of liquid is added and the pan is covered to keep in the steam. When a tender meat is relatively small, as with these pork chops, the braising goes quickly. The meat stays moist and tender, and the seasoned, reduced braising liquid contributes deep flavor to the sauce.

In a small saucepan, combine the apricots, cranberries, apple cider, and ½ cup (4 fl oz/125 ml) water. Bring to a boil over high heat. Remove from the heat and let the fruit soften for 10 minutes.

In a large sauté pan over medium-high heat, melt 2 tablespoons of the butter. Add the leeks and sauté until softened and lightly browned, about 5 minutes. Add the pear and sauté until nicely coated, 2–3 minutes longer. Add the softened dried fruits with their soaking liquid and the stock. Reduce the heat to medium and bring to a simmer. Cook until slightly thickened, about 5 minutes longer. Season to taste with salt and pepper. Set the sauce aside.

In a large sauté pan over medium-high heat, melt the remaining 1 tablespoon butter with the olive oil. Pat the pork chops dry with paper towels and season with salt and pepper. Add to the pan and cook until brown on the first side, about 2 minutes. Turn the chops and continue cooking on the second side until browned, about 2 minutes longer. Transfer to a platter and cover loosely with aluminum foil to keep warm.

Pour the drippings off the pan and discard. Add the apple brandy to the pan and heat over medium heat, scraping up the browned bits on the bottom of the pan with a wooden spoon. Add the reserved fruit sauce and mustard and bring to a simmer. Cook, stirring, until the alcohol has burned off, about 3 minutes. Taste and adjust the seasoning.

Return the pork chops to the pan and spoon over the sauce. Reduce the heat to medium-low and braise, covered, turning once, until the pork is just cooked through, about 10 minutes total. Garnish with the parsley and serve immediately on warmed plates.

MAKES 6 SERVINGS

1 cup (6 oz/185 g) diced dried apricots

½ cup (2 oz/60 g) dried cranberries

1 cup (8 fl oz/250 ml) apple cider

3 tablespoons unsalted butter

2 leeks, white and light green parts only, cleaned (page 13) and finely chopped

1 firm yet ripe pear, peeled, cored, and cut into 1-inch (2.5-cm) dice

1 cup (8 fl oz/250 ml) beef or chicken stock (page 112) or prepared broth

Salt and freshly ground pepper

2 tablespoons olive oil

6 bone-in center-cut pork chops, about 1½–2 inches (4–5 cm) thick

½ cup (4 fl oz/125 ml) apple brandy

2 teaspoons whole-grain mustard

2 tablespoons finely chopped fresh flat-leaf (Italian) parsley

VEAL BLANQUETTE WITH WILD MUSHROOMS

1 sprig fresh flat-leaf (Italian) parsley, plus chopped parsley for garnish

1 sprig fresh thyme

1 bay leaf

1 clove garlic, sliced

1 tablespoon peppercorns

3 lb (1.5 kg) boneless veal shoulder or veal stewing meat, cut into 2-inch (5-cm) pieces

4 cups (32 fl oz/1 l) chicken stock (page 112) or prepared veal or chicken broth

1 yellow onion, cut into quarters

Salt and freshly ground pepper

½ lb (250 g) fresh pearl onions, blanched and peeled (page 18), or frozen pearl onions, thawed

3 tablespoons unsalted butter

6 oz (185 g) chanterelle or other fresh wild mushrooms

1 tablespoon all-purpose (plain) flour

¼ cup (2 fl oz/60 ml) heavy (double) cream

Bundle the parsley sprig, thyme, bay leaf, garlic, and peppercorns in a square of cheesecloth (muslin) and tie with kitchen string to make a bouquet garni *(right)*. In a large saucepan, combine the veal, stock, onion quarters, garlic, bouquet garni, and salt and pepper to taste. Bring to a boil over high heat, then reduce the heat to low, cover, and cook gently until the veal is just tender, about 1¼ hours. Discard the bouquet garni and onion quarters.

Add the pearl onions to the pan and simmer until the onions are tender, 10–15 minutes longer. Using a slotted spoon, transfer the veal and onions to a bowl. Bring the cooking liquid to a boil over high heat and cook until reduced to about 2 cups (16 fl oz/500 ml), about 10 minutes.

Meanwhile, in a frying pan over medium heat, melt 2 tablespoons of the butter. Add the mushrooms and salt and pepper to taste and sauté until tender, about 5 minutes. Set aside.

In a small bowl, mash together the remaining 1 tablespoon butter with the flour, blending to make a smooth paste. Gradually whisk the butter mixture into the simmering stock, a little at a time. When all of the mixture has been added, simmer until slightly thickened, whisking constantly, about 2 minutes longer.

Return the veal and pearl onions to the sauce and add the mushrooms. Simmer for 2 minutes to allow the flavors to blend. Add the cream and return to a simmer. Taste and adjust the seasoning.

Ladle into warmed bowls and serve, garnished with the parsley.

Serving Tip: Serve over steamed white rice or with mashed potatoes.

MAKES 6 SERVINGS

BOUQUET GARNI

Typically made from parsley, thyme, and bay leaves, this bundle of aromatic herbs is a frequent addition to French soups and stews. Peppercorns can be added to give a subtle bite to the finished dish. The herbs are tied together or wrapped in cheesecloth so they can be easily removed after cooking. To make a bouquet garni, place the herbs and peppercorns in the center of a square of cheesecloth, bring up the corners, and tie securely with kitchen string.

BRAISED SHORT RIBS WITH BEER

SHORT RIBS

Short ribs, typically cut from the chuck, are usually sold cut into 3-inch sections. Boneless or bone-in, short ribs are fatty and flavorful, making them a good choice for stews and braises. Short ribs are enjoying a renaissance on restaurant menus these days, as diners rediscover their comforting, homey flavor and succulent texture. They tend to shrink as they braise, making it easy to separate the meat from the bones when serving. A long, slow cooking breaks down the tough connective tissue and leaves the meat fork-tender and juicy.

Preheat the oven to 325°F (165°C).

Pat the ribs dry with paper towels and season with salt and pepper. In a large frying pan over medium-high heat, heat 2 tablespoons of the oil. Working in batches to avoid overcrowding the pan, add the ribs and brown on all sides, 7–10 minutes for each batch. Using a slotted spoon, remove each batch as it's finished and drain briefly on paper towels, then place in a large Dutch oven or heavy flameproof casserole.

In the same frying pan over medium-high heat, heat the remaining 1 tablespoon oil. Add the onions and sauté until browned, 7–10 minutes, stirring frequently and watching carefully so that they brown but do not burn. Add the carrots and sauté until softened, 2–3 minutes longer. Add the garlic and cook for 1 minute longer. Add the tomatoes, beer, and mustard. Season to taste with salt and pepper. Raise the heat to high and simmer for 1 minute to allow the flavors to blend. Pour the tomato sauce mixture over the short ribs and stir to combine.

Bake, covered, until the meat is very tender, 2¼–3 hours, turning the ribs every 45 minutes during the cooking time. Taste and adjust the seasoning.

Transfer the ribs to a serving platter, spoon over the sauce, and serve immediately.

Note: This dish is even better when made a day ahead. Refrigerate overnight, then remove the fat layer with a large spoon or spatula and reheat the short ribs gently.

Serving Tip: These short ribs pair perfectly with mashed potatoes.

MAKES 6 SERVINGS

5 lb (2.5 kg) lean beef short ribs, cut into 3-inch (7.5-cm) pieces

Salt and freshly ground pepper

3 tablespoons vegetable oil

3 large yellow onions, sliced thickly into rings

4 carrots, peeled and cut into slices ½ inch (12 mm) thick

4 cloves garlic, minced

1 cup (8 oz/250 g) canned crushed tomatoes

1½ cups (12 fl oz/375 ml) good-quality beer

1 teaspoon Dijon mustard

BEEF STROGANOFF

3 tablespoons olive oil

1½ lb (750 g) top sirloin, cut into thin strips about 1 inch (2.5 cm) wide and 2 inches (5 cm) long

Salt and freshly ground pepper

3 tablespoons unsalted butter

3 leeks, white and light green parts only, cleaned (page 13) and finely chopped

1 lb (500 kg) cremini mushrooms, brushed clean and sliced

1 tablespoon tomato paste

2 tablespoons all-purpose (plain) flour

2¼ cups (18 fl oz/560 ml) beef stock (page 112) or prepared broth

⅓ cup (3 oz/90 g) crème fraîche *(far right)*

2 teaspoons Dijon mustard

2 teaspoons fresh lemon juice

Finely chopped fresh flat-leaf (Italian) parsley for garnish

In a large frying pan over high heat, heat 1 tablespoon of the olive oil. Pat the beef dry with paper towels and season with salt and pepper. Add half of the beef strips, making sure not to crowd the pan, and sauté until nicely browned but still a little pinkish on both sides, about 1 minute per side. Transfer to a bowl. Repeat with another 1 tablespoon olive oil and the remaining meat.

In the same pan over medium heat, melt the butter with the remaining 1 tablespoon olive oil. Add the leeks and sauté until softened and lightly browned, about 5 minutes. Add the mushrooms and sauté until nicely browned, about 5 minutes longer. Season to taste with salt and pepper.

Stir in the tomato paste and cook until blended in, about 1 minute. Sprinkle the flour over the vegetables and stir to incorporate. Raise the heat to high, add the stock, and bring to a boil, scraping up the browned bits on the bottom of the pan with a wooden spoon. Let boil for 1 minute, then reduce the heat to medium. Add the crème fraîche, mustard, and lemon juice and cook for 1 minute longer to allow the flavors to blend. Taste and adjust the seasoning. Return the meat and any accumulated juices to the pan and cook just until the beef is heated through, about 2 minutes. Garnish with the parsley and serve immediately.

Serving Tip: Stroganoff, though not technically a braise, has a similar consistency when finished. It is traditionally served over wide egg noodles.

MAKES 6 SERVINGS

CRÈME FRAÎCHE

Crème fraîche is similar to sour cream but milder and sweeter, with a touch of nuttiness. Unlike sour cream, it can be simmered in sauces without curdling. Look for crème fraîche at well-stocked supermarkets or at gourmet food stores. To make your own, combine 1 cup (8 fl oz/250 ml) of nonultrapasteurized heavy (double) cream and 1 tablespoon buttermilk in a saucepan and heat over medium-low heat until just lukewarm. Pour into a bowl, cover loosely, and let stand at room temperature until thickened, 8–48 hours or more. Chill before using.

BRAISED OXTAILS WITH OLIVES

In a large soup pot over medium heat, heat the olive oil. Pat the oxtails dry with paper towels and season with salt and pepper. Working in batches to avoid crowding, add the meat and brown it on all sides, 4–5 minutes per batch. Transfer the oxtails to a bowl and set aside.

Add the onion, carrots, and bacon to the drippings in the pot and sauté over medium heat until the onions are softened and the bacon is lightly browned, about 10 minutes. Add the garlic and cook for 1 minute longer. Return the oxtails, along with any accumulated juices, to the pot. Add the stock, wine, tomatoes with their juice, bay leaf, thyme, anchovy paste, and salt and pepper to taste. Raise the heat to high and bring to a boil. Reduce the heat to low and simmer until the oxtails are very tender and the meat pulls away from the bone easily, about 3 hours, using a slotted spoon or skimmer to occasionally skim off any foam that rises to the surface.

Add the olives and vinegar and cook for 1 minute to allow the flavors to blend. Discard the bay leaf. Taste and adjust the seasoning. Skim any fat off the top. Transfer to a serving bowl and garnish with the parsley. Serve at once, or refrigerate overnight, skim off the fat from the top, and reheat before serving the next day.

MAKES 4–6 SERVINGS

OXTAILS

"Oxtails"—which nowadays come from steer and not oxen—are usually sold sliced crosswise into 2-inch (5-cm) portions. Like short ribs, they are experiencing a rediscovery of sorts, as more people come to appreciate them as a traditional comfort food. Long, slow cooking mellows the meat and releases the gelatin from the bones, making an extraordinarily savory stew. Since the meat tends to be fatty, make this dish a day ahead so you can skim the chilled fat off the top before reheating and serving.

2 tablespoons olive oil

4 lb (2 kg) oxtails, trimmed and cut into 2-inch (5-cm) pieces by the butcher

Salt and freshly ground pepper

1 large yellow onion, sliced

2 carrots, peeled and thinly sliced

¼ lb (125 g) thick-cut bacon, cut into strips ¼ inch (6 mm) wide

3 cloves garlic, minced

3 cups (24 fl oz/750 ml) beef stock (page 112) or prepared broth

2 cups (16 fl oz/500 ml) dry white wine

One 14½-oz (455-g) can diced tomatoes, with juice

1 bay leaf

½ teaspoon dried thyme

1 teaspoon anchovy paste

1 cup (5 oz/155 g) chopped pitted Kalamata olives (page 77)

2 tablespoons red wine vinegar

2 tablespoons finely chopped fresh flat-leaf (Italian) parsley

SOUP & STEW BASICS

Simmering on the stove top, a pot of soup or stew perfumes the house with the promise of a satisfying homemade meal. From an elegant first course to a hearty weekday supper, these dishes bring out the flavors of seasonal ingredients or convenient year-round pantry staples with aplomb. Soups, stews, and braises are wonderfully versatile and easily mastered. Soups have the most liquid, followed by stews. Braises reduce the liquid still further, surrounding larger pieces of meat, chicken, or fish with just enough liquid to produce a moist and tender dish in a reduced, flavorful sauce.

MAKING SOUP

Soups adapt to many roles on the dining table. A creamy winter squash and apple bisque can be an impressive first course for a holiday dinner party, while a hearty pot of split pea soup makes a cozy winter supper. Cool vichyssoise perks up summer appetites, and a bowl of chicken and rice soup is perhaps the ultimate comfort food.

MAKING STOCK

A well-made savory stock is the foundation of a good soup, turning even the simplest recipe into a memorable meal. The base of a stock is water simmered with meat, chicken, or fish and its bones or shells. Light stocks can be made from vegetables alone. Stocks are usually seasoned with aromatics, such as onions, celery, garlic, and herbs and spices, which often include bay leaves, parsley, and peppercorns. Inexpensive parts of meat—meaty beef bones, chicken thighs, neck bones—are the best choices for making stock, as the long simmering releases their rich flavor and natural gelatin into the stock.

It takes only a little planning to have a freezer full of ready-to-use stock. As you cook throughout the week, tuck extra bones, scraps, and shells into lock-top freezer bags and stash in the freezer. (Lobster, shrimp, and crab shells are particularly good for seafood stocks.) When you've collected enough to make a full pot of stock, it will only take about 20 minutes of active work to put together your stock.

Always let stock cool to room temperature before transferring it to the refrigerator or freezer. Stock can be stored, covered, in the refrigerator for up to 3 days. Otherwise, divide it into 2- and 4-cup (16– and 32–fl oz/500-ml and 1-l) portions, pour it into plastic storage containers, and store in the freezer for up to 3 months. Remember that liquids expand slightly as they freeze, so leave a small amount of room at the top of any container.

USING PREPARED BROTH

There are times, of course, when making stock isn't an option. If you are buying prepared stock, generally labeled "broth," choose a high-quality brand of canned, concentrated, or frozen broth. Read the ingredients and try to find a brand made with real meat, chicken, and vegetables rather than mainly salt, fat, and chemical flavorings. Canned broth can be extremely salty; for best results, look for low-sodium brands.

You can also "doctor" canned broth by simmering it with a quartered onion, a halved carrot and celery stalk, and fresh herbs. Recently, more gourmet markets have begun to sell frozen homemade stock, which is a nice option. Bottled clam juice can be substituted for fish stock. Always add salt sparingly and taste for seasoning when using prepared broths.

PURÉEING

Partially or completely puréeing a soup can give it a robust texture or smooth consistency and is called for in many of the recipes in this book. Different ingredients provide soup with sufficient body to be puréed: root vegetables such as potatoes or carrots; squash; tomatoes; bread crumbs; or cooked grains such as rice or corn.

USING A STANDING BLENDER

Blenders make puréeing soups fast and easy. They usually can handle more liquid volume than food processors, and they are sometimes more suitable than food processors for puréeing because they more fully break down the fibers found in some vegetables. When using a blender, work in small batches, and start with the lowest speed. Gradually increase the speed until the desired consistency is reached. Always hold the lid on tight to prevent hot liquid from spattering.

USING A HANDHELD BLENDER

Handheld blenders, also called immersion blenders, have a blade that can be lowered directly into a pot of soup, blending large amounts of soup at a time with little mess. They also tend to incorporate more air into a liquid and can be used to make frothy foam on creamed soups. Immerse the blade completely before turning on the blender to prevent spattering.

USING A FOOD MILL

A hand-cranked food mill purées soup by forcing ingredients through a perforated conical disk, which functions something like a sieve, removing fibers, skins, and seeds from vegetables like asparagus, corn, and tomatoes. Food mills tend to give a more even texture than food processors. Most mills come with both medium and fine disks, offering the cook a choice of coarser or smoother purées.

USING A FOOD PROCESSOR

A food processor purées soups almost instantaneously. First, fit the processor with the metal blade. Ladle a small batch of the cooked solids and a bit of the liquid into the food processor's bowl, being careful not to overfill. Close and pulse the machine several times, then process until the purée is the desired consistency. Take care to purée hot soups in small batches to avoid spattering.

When puréeing soup in a food processor, straining may be necessary to remove fibers, skins, or seeds. Remove them by pouring the purée into a sieve set over a large bowl. Using the back of a spoon, press the purée through the sieve, discarding any solids trapped in the wire mesh. Repeat in batches with the remaining purée. Stir to give the purée an even consistency, returning it to the pan if necessary for gentle reheating.

MAKING STEW

Stews lie at the heart of many cuisines, and with good reason: They are delicious and versatile, turning tough but flavorful cuts of meat into meltingly tender forkfuls, or melding an assortment of fish and shellfish into an aromatic dish infused with the essence of the sea. Beans and grains can be employed to make filling, flavorful meatless stews, spiced with any number of flavors from around the world. Using less liquid than a soup but more than a braise, stews surround bite-sized bits of meat, fish, or vegetables with a savory, saucelike broth, which generally cooks (stews) for a long time to mellow and meld all of the flavors and tenderize the meat.

Stews can be cooked either on the stove top or in the oven, as long as the heat can be regulated and the stew kept at a slow simmer. Always use a heavy pot with a cover—such as an enameled cast-iron Dutch oven—to ensure slow, even cooking of stews without scorching. Quick-cooking vegetables such as peas or leafy fresh herbs like basil or cilantro should be added at the end of cooking to preserve their color and flavor.

CUTS OF MEAT FOR STEWING

Flavor, rather than tenderness, is what you should look for in choosing cuts of meat for stewing. The long cooking will break down any tough connective tissues and fibers. Though boneless meat is more common, meat on the bone is also an option; the bones will enrich the stew and can be removed after cooking. Beef round or chuck makes the best stewing beef, while lamb shoulder or shank is often used for lamb stews.

Although supermarkets sell packages of precut stewing meat, you'll get higher-quality meat if you buy a single cut and ask the butcher to cube it (or cube it yourself). For poultry, chicken thighs and duck legs are good choices for stewing; their robust flavor and succulent texture adapt well to long cooking. Seafood stews generally use a mix of shellfish—for example, shrimp, mussels, and crab—and/or firm-fleshed white fish such as sea bass or halibut.

DEGLAZING

Stew and braise recipes often call for the meat to be browned in batches before being cooked in liquid; this step will boost the color and flavor of the finished dish. Deglazing, a classic French technique, calls for scraping up the delicious browned bits from the bottom of the pan after sautéing. To deglaze, add a small amount of liquid such as wine, stock, or vinegar to the pan and bring it to a boil over high heat. As the liquid boils, scrape the bottom of the pan with a wooden spoon to dislodge any browned bits stuck to the bottom of the pan. Continue cooking to reduce the liquid, thereby adding a level of complexity to the stew's aroma.

OTHER TECHNIQUES

MAKING A ROUX

Made from flour stirred into melted butter or warmed oil, a roux adds depth of flavor and a thicker consistency to a soup or stew. To make a roux, over medium heat, melt the butter or heat the oil. Stir in the flour a little at a time, stirring constantly with a whisk as you cook to the desired color. The roux must cook long enough so that the flour loses its raw flavor but not so much as to scorch (usually 3–4 minutes for a light roux, 5–7 minutes for a darker roux). When stock is added to a roux, the resulting thick liquid is called a velouté. Both roux and velouté serve as the backbone of numerous traditional European soups and stews.

SOAKING BEANS

Before soaking beans, pick them over and remove any small stones or other debris. Submerge beans in cold water, removing any that float to the surface. Drain and rinse. Place beans in a large container and add enough cold water to cover them by several inches. Let soak at room temperature for at least 4 hours or overnight.

Alternatively, use the quick-soak method: Put the beans in a deep pot, cover with water by several inches, and bring to simmer. Remove the pot from the heat, cover, and let stand for about 1 hour.

PEELING AND SEEDING TOMATOES

First carve a shallow X in the blossom end of each tomato. Bring a saucepan of water to a boil. Immerse the tomatoes, in batches if necessary, until the skins begin to wrinkle, 15–30 seconds (longer if the tomatoes are very firm and not quite ripe). Remove the tomatoes with a strainer or slotted spoon and let cool. Slip off the peels and discard. To seed, cut each tomato in half crosswise and lightly squeeze or shake it to remove the seeds.

CLEANING MUSSELS

To clean mussels, scrub the grit off the shells with a stiff-bristled brush. Remove the beard (the little tuft of fibers used by the mussel to connect itself to rocks or pilings) by cutting or scraping it off using a knife or scissors. (Removing the beard kills the mussel, so do not debeard mussels more than an hour before cooking.) Always discard any mussels that feel very light or do not close to the touch, as they're probably dead and may be filled with sand or grit. After cooking, discard any mussels that fail to open.

WORKING WITH CUCUMBERS

"Slicing" cucumbers are the smooth, slender dark green vegetables that regularly show up in green salads, on crudité platters, and as a garnish on cold plates. They are available in two varieties: outdoor and English, or hothouse. Outdoor varieties should be 8–10 inches (20–25 cm) long and 1–1½ inches (2.5–4 cm) in diameter, and they are often coated with wax. Avoid waxed cucumbers if possible, as waxed skin must be peeled, and with the skin goes the vitamin A. English cucumbers are usually 12–16 inches (30–40 cm) long. They tend to be less bitter, and have thin skin. They are virtually seedless.

When using cucumber in a chilled soup, peel off the skin with a vegetable peeler, then cut the cucumber in half lengthwise. Use a melon baller or spoon to scoop out the seeds and the surrounding pulpy matter, and slice crosswise to the desired thickness.

MAKING BRAISES

Braising is a gentle, moist-cooking technique that can be applied to any meat or vegetable, although it is most often used for large, tough cuts of meat (or smaller cuts with the bone in). An initial browning adds flavor, followed by long, slow cooking over low heat in a small amount of liquid—often wine or stock—not more than halfway up the sides of the food. Diced aromatics such as onion, carrot, and celery are often added at the beginning of the braising process to add flavor.

Because braises often use a single piece of meat and do not require a lot of ongoing or last-minute attention, they are a good choice for entertaining. A large Dutch oven or other heavy-bottomed, covered pot or casserole is the best cookware choice for braising, as you can brown, cook, and serve the braise all in the same container, without worrying about scorching the bottom.

Shown opposite are the basic steps for braising meat:

1 Dredging and browning meat: Dredging the meat in flour seasoned with salt and pepper aids in browning and makes the final sauce thicker and more flavorful. First, dredge the meat in the seasoned flour, either in a large bowl or a lock-top plastic bag. Next, add the meat to hot oil in a pan in batches and brown on it all sides; don't overcrowd the pan, or the meat will steam rather than brown.

2 Deglazing: Deglazing releases the flavorful cooked bits from the bottom of the pan after browning. After removing the meat, add a small amount of wine, stock, or other liquid to the pan. Bring to a simmer and scrape up any residue from the bottom of the pan with a wooden spoon.

3 Adding liquid: Add liquid (often a mixture of broth and wine seasoned with spices and herbs) to the pan, using just enough to come one-third to halfway up the sides of the meat. This small amount of liquid encourages the braise to cook, slowly, in a mixture of steam and its own juices, while preventing it from scorching or sticking to the pan. Turning the meat once during cooking helps all sides to cook evenly.

4 Reducing the sauce: Once the meat is done braising, if the cooking liquid still seems thin or watery, remove the meat, then bring the liquid to a boil over high heat and simmer quickly to concentrate it to a saucelike consistency.

BASIC RECIPES

Here are some of the basic preparations that are integral to recipes in this collection.

CHICKEN STOCK

4 fresh flat-leaf (Italian) parsley sprigs

1 fresh thyme sprig

1 bay leaf

6 lb (3 kg) chicken necks and backs

3 stalks celery, halved

3 carrots, peeled and halved

2 yellow onions, halved

2 leeks, white and light green parts only, cleaned (page 13) and sliced

Salt and freshly ground pepper

Wrap the parsley, thyme, and bay leaf in a piece of cheesecloth (muslin) and secure with kitchen string to make a bouquet garni.

In a large stockpot, combine the bouquet garni, chicken, celery, carrots, onions, and leeks. Add enough cold water to just cover the ingredients (about 14 cups/3.5 l). Slowly bring to a boil over medium heat. Reduce the heat to as low as possible and let simmer, uncovered, for 3 hours, skimming off the foam that rises to the surface. Taste and season with salt and pepper.

Strain the stock into a bowl through a fine-mesh sieve. Let cool. Pour into airtight containers and refrigerate for at least 30 minutes or up to overnight. Remove the hardened fat from the surface and discard, then refrigerate for up to 3 days or freeze for up to 3 months. Makes about 3 qt (3 l).

MEAT STOCK

6 lb (3 kg) beef or veal shank bones with some meat on them, cut into 3-inch (7.5-cm) lengths by the butcher

2 yellow onions, coarsely chopped

4 fresh flat-leaf (Italian) parsley sprigs

1 fresh thyme sprig

1 bay leaf

2 carrots, peeled and coarsely chopped

1 stalk celery, coarsely chopped

Salt and freshly ground pepper

Preheat the oven to 425°F (220°C). Put the bones and onions in a lightly oiled roasting pan and roast until well browned, 35–40 minutes.

Wrap the parsley, thyme, and bay leaf in a piece of cheesecloth (muslin) and secure with kitchen string to make a bouquet garni.

In a large stockpot, combine the bones, onions, carrots, celery, bouquet garni, and 8 qt (8 l) water and bring to a boil over high heat. Reduce the heat to low and skim the foam from the top. Simmer, uncovered, for at least 3 hours or up to 6 hours. Taste and season with salt and pepper.

Strain the stock through a fine-mesh sieve into another container and discard the solids. Let cool. Cover and refrigerate until the fat solidifies. Discard the congealed fat. Pour into airtight containers and refrigerate for up to 3 days or freeze for up to 3 months. Makes about 5 qt (5 l).

VEGETABLE STOCK

2 yellow onions, coarsely chopped

2 leeks, white and green parts, cleaned (page 13) and sliced

4 stalks celery with leaves, chopped

4 carrots, peeled and coarsely chopped

1 red potato, diced

¼ lb (125 g) mushrooms, quartered

6 cloves garlic

8 fresh flat-leaf (Italian) parsley stems

2 bay leaves

8 whole peppercorns

Salt

In a large stockpot, combine the onions, leeks, celery, carrots, potato, mushrooms, garlic, parsley, bay leaves, and peppercorns. Add enough cold water to just cover the ingredients (about 10 cups/2.5 l). Bring to a boil over high heat, then reduce the heat to medium-low and let simmer, uncovered, for 1½ hours, using a spoon or skimmer to regularly skim off the foam that rises to the surface. Taste and season with salt.

Strain the stock through a fine-mesh sieve into a large bowl. Press on the vegetables with the back of a spoon to extract as much of the flavor as possible. Let the stock cool to room temperature. Pour into airtight containers and refrigerate for up to 3 days or freeze for up to 3 months. Makes about 2 qt (2 l).

FISH STOCK

4 fresh flat-leaf (Italian) parsley sprigs

1 fresh thyme sprig

1 bay leaf

¼ cup (2 fl oz/60 ml) extra-virgin olive oil

1 yellow onion, coarsely chopped

1 carrot, peeled and coarsely chopped

2 stalks celery, coarsely chopped

½ cup (4 fl oz/125 ml) dry white wine

4 qt (4 l) water

2 lb (1 kg) fish bones and parts from white-fleshed fish

Wrap the parsley, thyme, and bay leaf in a piece of cheesecloth (muslin) and secure with kitchen string to make a bouquet garni.

In a large stockpot over medium heat, heat the olive oil. Add the onion, carrot, and celery and sauté until softened, 4–5 minutes. Add the wine and deglaze the pot, stirring to scrape up the browned bits from the bottom. Raise the heat to medium-high and cook until the wine is almost completely evaporated. Add the water, fish bones and parts, and bouquet garni and bring to a boil. Reduce the heat to low and simmer, uncovered, for 30 minutes.

Strain the stock through a fine-mesh sieve into another container and discard the solids. Let cool. Pour into airtight containers and refrigerate for up to 2 days or freeze for up to 2 months. Makes about 3 qt (3 l).

GARLIC TOASTS

6–8 slices French or Italian baguette, about ½ inch (12 mm) thick

Olive oil for brushing

1–2 cloves garlic, halved

Preheat the oven to 375°F (190°C). Arrange the bread slices in a single layer on a baking sheet. Brush with olive oil. Bake just until golden, 5–7 minutes, watching carefully that they don't burn. Remove from the oven and rub each toast with the cut side of a garlic clove. Makes 6–8 toasts.

BASIL PESTO

2 cloves garlic, halved

2 cups (2 oz/60 g) firmly packed fresh basil leaves, chopped if using a mortar and pestle

½ cup (½ oz/15 g) fresh flat-leaf (Italian) parsley leaves

2 tablespoons pine nuts

½ cup (4 fl oz/125 ml) extra-virgin olive oil

¾ cup (3 oz/90 g) freshly grated Parmesan cheese

Salt and freshly ground pepper

In a food processor or with a mortar and pestle, process or grind the garlic to a coarse paste. Add the basil, parsley, pine nuts, and olive oil and process or grind to a thick paste. Stir in the cheese and season with salt and pepper to taste. Makes about 1½ cups (12 fl oz/375 ml).

HOMEMADE MAYONNAISE

1 large egg

1 teaspoon Dijon mustard

1 teaspoon fresh lemon juice or white wine vinegar

Salt and freshly ground pepper

¾ cup (6 fl oz/180 ml) canola oil

¾ cup (6 fl oz/180 ml) olive oil

Place the uncracked egg in a bowl of hot tap water for 3 minutes to warm. In a blender or food processor, combine the egg, mustard, lemon juice, ½ teaspoon salt, and ¼ teaspoon pepper. In a glass pitcher, combine the canola and olive oils. With the motor running, slowly drizzle the combined oils into the blender (it should take at least 1 minute) to make a thick mayonnaise. Stir in 1 tablespoon hot water. Makes about 1¾ cups (14 fl oz/430 ml).

GLOSSARY

BELL PEPPERS, ROASTING You can roast peppers by holding them directly over a gas flame on a stove top or placing them in a broiler (grill). In either case, turn with tongs until the skin is blistered and blackened on all sides; be careful not to let the flesh burn. Put the blackened peppers into a paper bag, close tightly, and let stand for 10 minutes, then peel off the skin with your fingers. Slit the peppers lengthwise, remove the stems, seeds, and membranes, and cut as desired.

CAJUN SEASONING BLEND Cajun seasoning blend is a prepared mixture of spices—usually a combination of cayenne, paprika, chili powder, onion powder, cloves, and dried spices. It is available in most supermarkets.

CARAWAY SEEDS The seed of a member of the parsley family, the caraway seed has a strong, nutty taste that is closely identified with rye bread. Used throughout northern and central Europe, caraway seeds add rich flavor to meat and poultry dishes and stews. They are almost always used whole. Store them in an airtight container in a cool, dark place for up to 6 months.

CELLOPHANE NOODLES Also called mung bean, transparent, glass, or bean thread noodles, cellophane noodles are made from ground mung beans and water. They resemble thin white wires when dry but become soft and transparent after cooking. Soften the noodles in warm water for 20 minutes before adding them to soups or stir-fried noodle dishes. Deep-fried without soaking, they expand into a nest of puffy, white crisps.

CHEDDAR CHEESE A cow's milk cheese appreciated for its sharp, salty flavor, which ranges from mild to sharp. Farmhouse Cheddars taste stronger than other American Cheddars. Cheddar is made primarily in the United States, Canada, and the United Kingdom.

CHILES Here are some common chile types, used in the recipes in this book:

Chipotle: The smoked and dried version of jalapeños, chipotles are widely available canned with garlic, tomatoes, and vinegar and labeled "chipotles en adobo." They are moderately hot and have a distinctive smoky flavor.

Jalapeño: This bright green pepper, 1½ inches (4 cm) long, ranges from hot to very hot and is one of the most widely used in the United States. It is available canned or fresh and is sometimes seen in its bright-red ripe state.

Pasilla: Also called *chile negro*, this dried chile is dark, narrow, and wrinkled. About 6 inches (15 cm) long, pasillas are sweet and hot.

Thai: Small, thin green or red chiles, usually only about 1 inch (2.5 cm) long and very hot. Also known as bird chiles.

COUSCOUS Couscous is a type of pasta made from durum wheat (semolina). Homemade couscous is made by moistening semolina and rolling it between the palms of the hands to form tiny pellets. These are steamed until tender. Commercial couscous is quick cooking and available at most supermarkets and natural-food stores.

CUMIN This spice is characteristic in Mexican and Indian cooking and has a distinct aroma. Cumin is available in the spice section of supermarkets, either ground or as light brown seeds that can be toasted and ground. It should be used sparingly to enhance the flavors of meats and vegetables, not overwhelm them.

DIJON MUSTARD A sharply flavored prepared mustard from the Dijon area in France, Dijon mustard is made primarily from ground brown mustard seeds, white wine and/or white vinegar, and seasonings.

EGG, RAW Eggs are sometimes used raw or partially cooked in sauces and other preparations. These eggs run a risk of being infected with salmonella or other bacteria, which can lead to food poisoning. This risk is of most concern to small children, older people, pregnant women, and anyone who has a compromised immune system. If you have health and safety concerns, do not consume undercooked eggs.

FENNEL A bulb-shaped vegetable, fennel has a mild licorice flavor. The feathery fronds can be chopped and added to a dish as a seasoning or garnish, and the dried seeds are often featured in Mediterranean and Asian recipes. To prepare fennel, cut off the tops of the stalks where the fronds become dense, cut the bulb in half lengthwise, and cut out the solid core at the bottom of the bulb. Slice the fennel crosswise.

HORSERADISH CREAM This piquant combination of horseradish and sour cream can be bought at well-stocked supermarkets, or you can make your own by stirring together ½ cup sour cream with 2 tablespoons prepared horseradish.

LARDONS Simply the French word for "little pieces of fat," lardons refers to thin strips of pork fat, which are inserted into dry cuts of meat to make them more succulent and flavorful, or strips of bacon used in a salad or a rich braise.

MANDOLINE A mandoline is a flat, rectangular tool used for slicing food into very thin strips. They usually come an assortment of smooth and corrugated blades, so food can be sliced, julienned, or waffle-cut. The advantages of using a mandoline are precision and regularity.

PARSNIP A relative of the carrot, this ivory-colored root closely resembles its brighter, more familiar cousin. Parsnips have a slightly sweet flavor and a tough, starchy texture that softens with cooking. They are a staple of hearty winter braises, and are excellent roasted, steamed, boiled, or baked.

PORT A sweet and full-bodied fortified wine, Port is named for the place from which it was first shipped, the city of Porto in northern Portugal. Port is available in three types: sweet ruby Port, as red as its name; amber-colored, drier tawny Port; and the most expensive, vintage Port, which is rich and complex, and can be aged for decades.

RICE STICK NOODLES Rice sticks are a kind of flat, dried noodle made from rice. You'll find them at well-stocked supermarkets and Asian markets.

MIRIN An important ingredient in Japanese cuisine, mirin is a sweet cooking wine made by fermenting glutinous rice and sugar. The pale gold and syrupy wine adds a rich flavor and translucent sheen to sauces, dressings, grilled meats, and simmered dishes.

SESAME OIL, DARK Dark Asian sesame oil has a deep amber color and rich flavor reminiscent of toasted sesame seeds. Because of its strong flavor, it should be used in small amounts. Don't confuse it with the clear-pressed sesame seed oil sold in natural-food stores.

THAI BASIL In Thailand, basil is often combined with fresh mint for seasoning stir-fries and curries. The most common kind of Thai basil has tapered dark green leaves, often tinged with purple, and a distinct licorice flavor that sets it apart from Western basil.

TOMATOES, FIRE-ROASTED Using fire-roasted tomatoes gives dishes a deep, smoky edge that blends especially well with the Mexican flavors of cumin, chile, and cilantro. Canned fire-roasted tomatoes, which are produced by either open-fire roasting or hardwood smoking, are available in supermarkets and natural-foods stores.

INDEX

SIMON & SCHUSTER SOURCE
A division of Simon & Schuster, Inc.
Rockefeller Center
1230 Avenue of the Americas
New York, NY 10020

WILLIAMS-SONOMA
Founder and Vice-Chairman: Chuck Williams

WELDON OWEN INC.
Chief Executive Officer: John Owen
President and Chief Operating Officer: Terry Newell
Vice President, International Sales: Stuart Laurence
Creative Director: Gaye Allen
Series Editor: Sarah Putman Clegg
Editor: Emily Miller
Designer: Leon Yu
Design Assistant: Marisa Kwek
Production Director: Chris Hemesath
Color Manager: Teri Bell
Shipping and Production Coordinator: Todd Rechner

Weldon Owen wishes to thank the following people for
their generous assistance and support in producing this
book: Contributing Writer Stephanie Rosenbaum; Copy
Editor Carrie Bradley; Consulting Editor Carolyn Miller;
Production Designer Joan Olsen; Food and Prop Stylists Kim
Konecny and Erin Quon; Photographer's Assistant Faiza Ali;
Assistant Food Stylist Michael Sorantino; Proofreaders
Arin Hailey and Sharron Wood; Indexer Ken DellaPenta.

Set in Trajan, Utopia, and Vectora.

Williams-Sonoma Collection *Soup & Stew* was
conceived and produced by Weldon Owen Inc.,
814 Montgomery Street, San Francisco,
California 94133, in collaboration with
Williams-Sonoma, 3250 Van Ness Avenue,
San Francisco, California 94109.

A Weldon Owen Production
Copyright © 2004 by Weldon Owen Inc. and
Williams-Sonoma, Inc.

SIMON & SCHUSTER SOURCE and colophon are
registered trademarks of Simon & Schuster, Inc.

For information regarding special discounts for
bulk purchases, please contact Simon & Schuster
Special Sales at 1-800-456-6798 or
business@simonandschuster.com

Color separations by Bright Arts Graphics
Singapore (Pte.) Ltd.
Printed and bound in Singapore by Tien Wah
Press (Pte.) Ltd.

First printed in 2004.

10 9 8 7 6 5 4 3 2 1

Library of Congress Cataloging-in-Publication
data is available.

ISBN 0-7432-6185-2

A NOTE ON WEIGHTS AND MEASURES

All recipes include customary U.S. and metric measurements. Metric conversions are based on
a standard developed for these books and have been rounded off. Actual weights may vary.